How To Develop
Competency-Based
Vocational Education

HOW TO DEVELOP
COMPETENCY-BASED
VOCATIONAL
EDUCATION

by William G. Perry, Jr.
Director, Collier County Area
Vocational-Technical Center
Naples, Florida

Prakken Publications, Inc.
Ann Arbor, Michigan

*For Sharon, Michael, and Jennifer whose
countless personal sacrifices made this book
possible.*

Library of Congress Catalog Card No. 82-80093
ISBN: 0-911168-48-6

Printed in the United States of America.
Second printing, 1984.
Third printing, 1988.

All photographs appear courtesy of *School Shop*
magazine unless otherwise noted.

Foreword

This book was written to help technical educators create competency-based instruction systems that develop employable skills in their students. The methods suggested in this book have been used successfully to convert occupational instruction programs to competency-based systems from more traditional approaches. The specific techniques that are described were synthesized by the author and have been used by many instructors.

The reader is guided through a curriculum revision process that is based on identifying skill proficiences that are suited to the needs of employers. *How to Develop Competency-Based Vocational Education* concentrates on the components that must be included in the conversion.

The first step in this process is the selection of an occupation that has a high demand in the instructor's service area. A systematic approach is used to develop a comprehensive list of the broad sets of skills and knowledge that are required of entry-level employees. The reader is then guided through a process which focuses on the development of competency statements that include measurable standards. Methods for describing performance goals in such a way that they reflect the minimum acceptable standards to obtain and maintain employment are discussed.

Sound principles of learning are used to identify instructional units and create a course outline for a job title curriculum that proceeds from the simple to the complex. The final stage in the sequence involves the development of learning activities designed to help students obtain prestated occupational goals. Principles and methods of techno-motor skill instruction are also presented.

How to Develop Competency-Based Vocational Education is a complete teacher-centered manual for creating a valid and accountable competency-based curriculum for technical instruction. Readers who follow the suggestions in this text are sure to improve the quality of their occupational instruction program and enhance the employability of their students.

How To Develop
Competency-Based
Vocational Education

The Competency-Based Instruction System

A competency-based instruction system greatly increases the likelihood of adequately preparing students for employment. This, of course, is a major objective of vocational education, but establishing such a system is rather complex and sometimes difficult. Nevertheless, the effort is well spent in terms of doing a better job of preparing your students for work and the personal satisfaction of having concrete evidence of attaining this goal. This book will outline the techniques necessary for achieving positive results.

This introductory chapter will answer the following questions about competency-based instruction systems:

What is an occupational competency?

What is a competency-based instruction system?

Why should you consider designing and using a
  competency-based instruction system?

What will it cost to develop this type of system?

What Is an Occupational Competency?

Webster defines the term *competency* as the state or quality of being capable; it can also mean an ability or skill possessed by an individual. An *occupational* competency must include the objective of marketability; the skill must be of such a nature that an employer is willing to pay for its performance. The development of marketable skills is central to all fields of vocational-technical education. Therefore, an *occupational competency* can be defined as:

> A specific job skill that an employer expects an employee to possess in order to obtain and maintain employment.

Thousands of examples of competencies can easily be listed by instructors. Consider your own past work experience and recall the skills that you possessed or developed in order to function in a manner that pleased your employer. Those skills were competencies. Consider the following situations.

Certain proficiencies related to the growth of turf grass, for example, are likely to be required of groundskeepers at a local country club. One of the competencies expected of an entry-level worker may be expressed by the employer as follows:

> The people who work for us as groundskeepers must know about the various types of fertilizers to be used on each area of the golf course.

The employer may expect the worker to possess other specialized skills which could be considered occupational competencies. For example:

> Groundskeepers at Sunny Dale Golf and Country Club must know how to remove and replace the major engine components on 2- and 4-cycle engine lawn maintenance equipment.

Competencies, therefore, are the skills and sets of knowledge which an employer looks for in an employee who hopes to obtain and maintain employment. These sets of knowledge and skills may or may not be directly related to the individual's primary job function.

I recall a general sales clerk position in which one of the competencies required by the employer was the ability to arrange shirts correctly on a shelf in alternating layers and by size. Another requirement in this job was the ability to accurately calculate markup, to arrange pricing characters on the printing machine, and to run price stickers for all incoming merchandise. An additional competency for this position was the sanitizing of the employees' restroom. The ability to perform this task had nothing to do with the preparation of merchandise for sale or with sales techniques, but it was required by this particular employer to maintain employment.

Since competency is a skill or set of knowledge that an employer wants an employee to possess, the instructor who wishes to design a competency-based instruction system must identify those skills associated with various job titles in a specific locale and describe them in terms that students can understand.

A partial list of competencies required by an employer of an entry-level welder might be stated by the instructor as follows:

> The student will achieve an "excellent" performance rating when demonstrating basic safety procedures and practices related to using electric arc welding equipment.

> The student will score 100 percent on an objective examination relating to the identification of the parts of an electric arc welding machine.

> The student will achieve an "above average" performance rating when demonstrating proficiency in the correct techniques for starting a weld, maintaining an arc, and restarting a weld.

> The student will achieve an "above average" performance rating when demonstrating proficiency in welding the following joints: butt corner, T-joint, and edge while using electric arc welding.

How to specify competencies in detail shall be discussed in a later chapter. It is sufficient to state at this point that the mission of occupational instruction is to develop certain competencies in students so that an employer will be willing to pay those individuals for the privilege of commanding their skilled service. Specific skills instruction for employment can best be imparted using a system of instruction with competencies as its basis.

What Is a Competency-Based Instruction System?

A competency-based instruction system is a specialized and systematic method of organizing occupational instruction. Central to a competency-based technique of instruction is the requirement that the majority of learning activities be centered on and keyed to the development of prestated job skills. These job skills are presented to students in a form which describes the levels of performance which are expected on the job. The core of a competency-based instruction *system* is that all activity in the shop and laboratory is focused on developing prestated occupational skills by using structured learning activities. The term *system* is italicized above to emphasize that a certain amount of management on the part of the instructor is

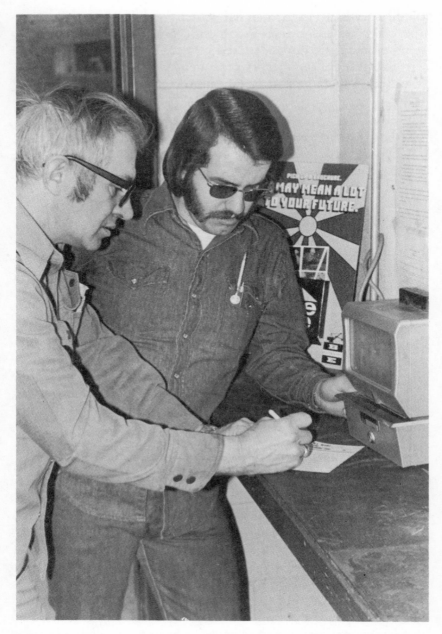

Illustration 1. To emphasize the importance of practical experience, this welding program used a time card to record attendance and student progress.

required to successfully implement and supervise competency-based instruction.

A competency-based instruction system has certain components which must be developed, structured, and managed effectively. They are:

Job title competencies
Organized learning activities
The organization of learning resources
Testing and evaluation of competency attainment
Competency recordkeeping

We will examine each of the parts of a competency-based instruction system briefly.

Job Title Competencies

The specific job for which a student is going to be prepared must be designated in a competency-based instruction system. This is the only way that the instructor can relate to the student the nature and purpose of the skills and knowledge which will be mastered. A vocational instructor could easily state, for example, that students were preparing for a career in horticulture by enrolling in a program called "Ornamental Horticulture." There is a difference, however, between teaching with a traditional course outline for horticulture and using the job title competency curriculum of "Landscape Designer/ Installer". The former is a course outline based on a course title, while the latter is the name of a specific occupation in which an individual can earn a living.

An instructor who is using a traditional vocational curriculum and wishes to convert to a program which is competency-based must decide for which job title students will be prepared. For each job title the instructor must then compile a detailed and well-researched list of skills or competencies which are representative of those required by local employers of an individual who works in that particular job classification. (Specialized methods of selecting viable job titles for which to develop competencies are discussed in Chapter 2.) One of the best ways to accomplish this is to actually consult with employers regarding what they expect of their employees.

The list of prestated skills should be written so that it leaves no doubt as to the actual level of proficiency required for each marketable skill. Occupational competency statements also specify the general conditions under which the student will demonstrate a skill as well as the level of performance. The italicized portion of the following competency statement illustrates this point.

> The student will achieve a "superior" performance rating *when demonstrating proficiency in the safe use of the radial arm saw.*

Each student who enrolls in a competency-based instruction program has presumably made an informed career selection. The comprehensive list of competencies which is developed for selected job titles becomes the basis for all instructional activities. Prior to beginning a program or unit of instruction, students should be aware of what competencies they must master. When approaching an organized learning activity, the mental attitude of students who have full knowledge of the skills to be learned and of what will be expected of them produces more positive results. The student accepts and understands the purpose of the learning activity because the skills to be gained to enhance employability have been clearly specified before the lesson is begun.

Most people will agree that using a method which spells out what must be learned and how well it must be mastered represents a strong stimulus for learning. You will read in later chapters how this principle of the psychology of learning sets the stage for the success of a competency-based instruction system.

Organized Learning Activities

One component which must be developed for competency-based instruction is a plan or method of assisting each student in mastering the list of skills associated with their chosen job title. The best approach is to structure learning activities. Competency-based instruction will follow naturally if the instructor has carefully organized the predetermined learning activities and experiences through which the students become technically accomplished. An example of an organized learning activity, in the form of a Learning Activities Package for a cosmetology class, is shown in Illustration 2. The organized learning activity specifies the competency which the student will be working on. The materials needed during the activity are listed, and students are guided through sequential steps designed to increase their skills and knowledge.

LEARNING ACTIVITIES PACKAGE 14
Sectioning

Competency to be met:

The student will achieve a minimum performance rating of "3" (on a scale of 0-5) when demonstrating proficiency in wetting, combing, and sectioning a mannequin for a haircut.

Materials Needed

1. Slide-tape series number 32-A
2. One slide-tape player
3. One mannequin
4. One comb
5. One spray bottle filled with water

Sequence of Learning Activities

1. Read pages 94-108 in your *Ajax Cosmetology* text where techniques for sectioning for a haircut are discussed.
2. View slide-tape series 32-A.
3. Take Self Test 14-1. Correct your examination. If you scored above 90 percent proceed to Learning Activity 4. Otherwise, reread the pages specified in Learning Activity 1 and discuss your original errors with the instructor before proceeding.
4. Secure your mannequin to a table top.
5. Spray the mannequin's head with water from the spray bottle as shown on the slide-tape series.
6. Proceed to section the hair as demonstrated in the slide-tape series. Compare your finished product with the various views provided in your textbook on pages 107-8. Comb out your sectioning and practice as many times as you feel necessary prior to proceeding to the next learning activity.
7. When you are ready to demonstrate initial competency attainment, call on your instructor.

Illustration 2. Learning Activities Package

The instructor's role is to manage student skill attainment through the use of organized learning activities. Each student is able to proceed at an individual pace. The instructor, as the learning manager, selects a training plan for an individual student which is appropriate for that student's level of skill achievement. For example, one student may be working on an organized learning activity relating to FCC licensure while another is working on basic semiconductor theory. The use of organized learning activities for competency attainment makes it possible for a large number of students to engage in various activities at the same time, according to their own unique proficiency level.

The use of organized learning activities in a competency-based instruction system eliminates traditional problems such as those that arise when an instructor announces to a group of 20 automotive mechanics students that they are going to learn how to adjust carburetors in a day's lesson. The learning inefficiency which results is well known to most industrial instructors. It would be difficult to arrange even a basic demonstration of how to adjust a carburetor so that 20 students could adequately observe it. Using organized learning activities which are designed to assist students in learning at their own rate is more effective and efficient.

Learning activities can assume many shapes and be structured in different fashions. For example:

> Learning Activities Packages
> Programmed learning materials
> 16mm films with review and activity sheets
> Controlled work station projects
> The reading of commercially printed materials
> The viewing of filmstrips, training loops, microfiche, or slide-
>   tape series
> Conducting a lecture/demonstration
> Videotapes
> Advanced hands-on projects

Organized learning activities are a necessary and beneficial component of a competency-based instruction system. They assist the instructor in controlling as many of the elements associated with the learning process as possible. Each organized learning activity centers on the development of specific skills and knowledge. The instructor arranges the sequence and timing of the activity so that the student approaches structured tasks in a maximum state of readiness. Materials, supplies, and equipment are used in a timely and efficient manner. Provisions for feedback are included and competency testing can be appropriately timed to increase student success.

Predetermined instructional activities collectively represent a strategy or plan whereby the student may become occupationally proficient. Every competency must have at least one learning activity as a basis on which to develop, but may have more than one learning activity associated with its attainment. To make effective use of a competency-based instruction system the instructor must carefully organize all learning resources.

The Organization of Learning Resources

Effective use of learning resources is characteristic of a competency-based instruction program. These learning resources can include:

Textbooks	Films and slides
Technical manuals	Video training cassettes
Parts manuals	Audiovisual equipment (e.g.,
Work stations	slide projectors, videotape
Supplies	recorders, cassette players)
Transparencies	Microfiche/tape series
Learning activities materials	Physical laboratory space

One purpose of organizing the use of learning resources is to assist all students in the time-efficient development of marketable skills. Some instructors may also need to organize carefully to compensate for limited accessibility to these resources in a particular program. An example of the effective use of learning resources is discussed below.

All available learning resources in the business education program of one secondary school are organized to simulate the required competencies of the various job titles which may be found in a business office. Learning resources have been structured within the classroom so that learning activities resemble a mail-order sales business.

A financial department accommodates several students. Desks, lights, calculators, and materials are carefully arranged within this area. The accounts receivable and accounts payable competencies, which are associated with basic bookkeeping, are developed at these work stations.

An "outside world" station stimulates all of the activity in the sales organization. This work station is occupied by a student whose primary function is to simulate written sales orders, payments, and correspondence coming into the business. Many advanced competencies associated with business correspondence, records management, and office systems are developed at this station by using a variety of selected learning resources.

Many other work stations exist in this sophisticated training model. Among them are office production work stations in which competencies associated with various job titles can be developed, such as office secretary, clerk-typist, receptionist, records manager, and office manager.

Students are even given the opportunity to explore advanced business-related competencies in other work stations. This is designed to develop an appreciation for the free enterprise system and a knowledge of the factors associated with the decision-making process and with production. This particular model includes work stations for such corporate positions as president, vice-president, and secretary-treasurer. All available learning resources are used in this classroom. They are organized so well that when the "outside world" station sends a letter to the company with a check representing payment on an account a complex chain of events is set in motion.

One student is responsible for opening and routing the mail. The payment is then carried to the accounting office where the payment is credited to the customer's account on the bookkeeping machine. A letter thanking the customer for payment is generated by the clerical work force and a new catalog of materials is forwarded to the customer. Various financial reports and sales figures are prepared at these work stations and sent to the corporate officers.

Numerous other functions could be included in this model. For example, another chain of events is triggered if an order comes into the office from the "outside world" station. Each learning activity in this simulated sales office is aimed at developing specific competencies. Learning resources are managed to maximize the students' opportunities to become more competent in the skills related to the jobs for which they are preparing.

You will recall that initially in a competency-based instruction system each student is given a copy of the job title competencies. Each of the prestated skills has at least one organized learning activity associated with its attainment, and the purpose of the learning activities is to develop these specific occupational proficiencies. To this end, the students may simply use a workbook, or they may work on an actual automobile engine which is mounted on a static rest stand. The relative progress of each student is of paramount importance in competency-based instruction. Therefore, the instructor's management of the many learning resources should be aimed at providing the student with appropriate experiences at precisely the time they are needed. Also, the resources must be carefully organized to insure accessibility.

Inefficiency would result if an instructor in a competency-based marine engine mechanics program, for example, decided to show the entire class in one day's lesson all of the videotapes on marine engines that had not been seen. Many students may not have the knowledge needed to appreciate viewing the tapes.

This type of mismanagement of learning resources is constantly aggravated in a case where there is only one videocassette recorder in the school. The instructor could make better use of time and resources if the use of the recorder and videotapes could be appropriately scheduled for the few students who would benefit from the viewing.

Other factors can affect the times when students should begin to pursue certain competencies. An instructor who has one student ready to be tested on competencies related to the building of a stud wall, for example, would be wise to wait for a short period of time until another student is ready to be tested on the same competency, simply because it would be extremely difficult for a single student to perform all of the tasks necessary to build and erect a 40-foot section of wall.

Many instructors who are developing competency-based instruction systems do not have all of the learning resources that are needed. Their use, therefore, must be intelligently managed within the framework of both their availability and the appropriate sequencing of each student's attempt to develop competencies. A well-organized competency testing and evaluation program will assist the instructor in making timely and effective decisions regarding the management of learning resources.

Testing and Evaluation of Competency Attainment

Effective testing and evaluation of competencies is so critical to the success of competency-based instruction that a later chapter is devoted entirely to this topic. For now, it is important only to state that competency testing and evaluation must also be carefully planned and directed. Central to a competency-based instruction system is the feature that both student and instructor know at all times precisely what is expected of the student in each learning situation. A detailed list of competencies, complete with statements regarding the desired levels of skill proficiency, is introduced at the very beginning of the student's program.

Competency statements are, in reality, tests. They are communicated to the student in terms of a desired level of skill performance. The following is an example of a competency statement for a health occupations program:

> The student will demonstrate proficiency in measuring a patient's blood pressure with 100 percent accuracy.

A test is underway, therefore, when a student makes an attempt to meet a specific competency level. There is immediate feedback as to the degree of success that the student has achieved.

Let's examine a typical example from a printing program:

> The student will demonstrate proficiency in adjusting the margins of an offset press to within 1/32 of an inch of the margins specified by the instructor.

The student is expected to show the instructor, under testing conditions, that all of the knowledge and skill which is necessary to make fine adjustments on the offset press has been mastered. The student will be told within moments whether the competency achievement level has been met. The instructor merely has to apply a ruler to the finished copy which is run on the press to determine if this competency has been met.

Instructors must also manage instructional time so that they will be in a position to "evaluate" their students' attempts at meeting competencies when they are prepared to be tested. Multiply the effort required to observe a single attempt to be tested on a competency by the size of a normal class and you can easily see that the instructor must know who is really ready to be tested, what should be observed, and when it needs to be done. There must not only be frequent opportunities for competency testing for all students, but also sufficient time for considered evaluation. Careful and reflective competency evaluation must take place.

A student may make an attempt at meeting a competency, achieve the stated performance standard, and still be evaluated by the

Illustration 3. Audiovisual teaching aids are often used to introduce information in competency-based occupational programs.

instructor as not yet having satisfactorily attained occupational proficiency. The student in question could have demonstrated, for example, a total disregard of prudent safety precautions while performing a critical task. The wise instructor would evaluate the student's performance as not being up to industrial standards. The same evaluation might properly be made if the student took too much time in completing the task relative to what might be expected on the job.

A student could conceivably need three weeks to develop proficiency in baking a particular kind of bread in order to meet a competency standard for a food services program. Because of the time factor, the instructor might require the student to successfully bake more than one loaf of the bread prior to "certifying" the student as competent.

The instructor must be familiar with the required standard of performance for employability for any given competency, and student performance must be evaluated in light of anticipated employment conditions and requirements. Remember that a competency is a test item, so the judgment of the instructor as to whether or not the observed student performance meets an employable standard is of great importance. Accurate and fair recordkeeping of competency testing and evaluation then becomes a tool for instructional management which helps to guide students through appropriate learning activities.

Competency Recordkeeping

Maintaining an accurate set of records for a competency-based instruction system is necessary for program effectiveness. The scores of students, plus a wide variety of other information, should be recorded in order to make the competency record a useful set of data for the instructor.

There are several specific reasons why the instructor must have an efficient recordkeeping system. One of the most important is that an effective method of tracking an individual student's progress can reduce the instructor's heavy management load. A good set of competency records allows the instructor to assess the relative performance of each student at a glance. Appropriate learning activities can then be selected on which the student can work.

Other reasons for maintaining an effective set of records are:

- The need to report student progress accurately
- The need to assess student performance instantly
- The need to provide a detailed transcript for use by employers
- The need to supply documented evidence for program accountability
- To use as a basis for prescriptive assignments
- To use as a basis for evaluating program effectiveness
- To use as a basis for evaluating student performance

A single record which contains the progress of each student's attempt at achieving occupational skill proficiency is critical in the use and management of a competency-based instruction system. One page of this record is shown in Illustration 4.

The competency record shown in this illustration is an example of one set of information which can be maintained on student performance. There is sufficient space in the first column for the identification number of the competency or a brief description of the skill to be attained. Immediately to the right is space for the minimum acceptable performance standard to be met. The student's actual score, once the competency has been attempted, is recorded in the next column. There is space in the following columns to write in the date and the instructor's comments.

COMPETENCY RECORD FOR

Program _____ _____ Job Title _____ Date _____

(Student Name)

COMPETENCY NUMBER OR DESCRIPTION	MINIMUM ACCEPTABLE PERFORMANCE	ACTUAL STUDENT PERFORMANCE	DATE OF ATTEMPT OR ATTAINMENT	INSTRUCTOR'S EVALUATIVE COMMENTS

Illustration 4. Student Progress Record

STUDENT'S PERMANENT ADDRESS:

_____
Name

_____
Street or Post Office Box

_____
City, State, Zip Code

_____
Area Code & Phone Number

PLACE OF INITIAL EMPLOYMENT:

_____
Name of Business

_____
Name of Employer or Supervisor

_____
Street or Post Office Box

_____
City, State, Zip Code

STATEMENT OF RELEASE

This statement authorizes the _____ to release information regarding my
Name of School

performance in _____ occupational instruction program to prospective employers.
Name of Program

_____
Signature of Student

_____
Signature of Parent or Guardian

Illustration 5. Student Information and Statement of Release

A student's progress record could contain other information, such as the student's permanent mailing address (for follow-up studies), current address, telephone number, date of enrollment, and other pertinent information. An example of an additional page which can be included in the progress record is shown in Illustration 5.

An additional feature included in this illustration is a waiver or "Statement of Release" of information. Federal laws which govern the use of records that are maintained on individuals in educational programs require that a statement of this kind be signed by the student and kept on file. The school could not otherwise provide this useful information to individuals wishing to assess the employability of a student. The statement indicates that the student, and the parent or guardian, if the student has not reached the age of majority, waive the right to maintain the confidentiality of the progress record. The student's competency record then becomes a transcript for the potential employer. This feature makes the record very meaningful to the student, and therefore it can function as a tremendous motivational device for student performance.

Some instructors find that a wall chart is another useful tool for organizing recordkeeping in a competency-based instruction system. This chart can serve as a simple day-to-day reference for the organization of instructional activity in the shop or laboratory. A sample of a wall chart for a competency-based instruction system is shown in Illustration 6.

Space is included across the top of the Competency Record Wall Chart to enter a description of each competency that is to be attained. There is also space for students' names on the left-hand side of the wall chart. Student progress can be assessed by the instructor or the student at a glance by referring to the key at the bottom of the chart. For example, a box which has been completely shaded in indicates that a particular student has completed the minimum level of required competence. A half-filled box indicates that the competency has been introduced and that the student is currently working on achieving the standard. A blank space means that the skill to be attained has yet to be introduced to the student.

Any system which is used in maintaining records for competency-based instruction ideally will indicate to the instructor what the student has done, at what level the student performed the various skills, and which competency the student should begin pursuing in the future.

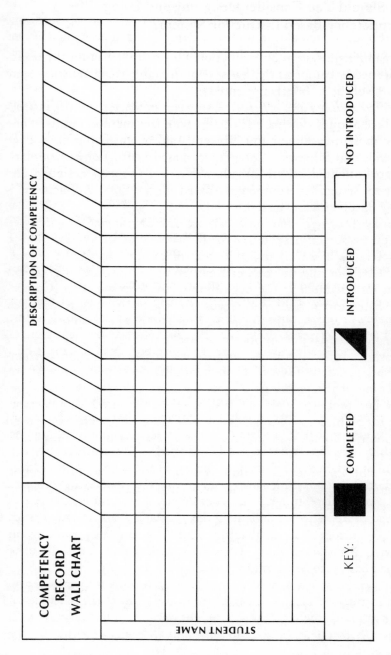

Illustration 6. Competency Record Wall Chart

Why Should You Consider Designing and Using a Competency-Based Instruction System?

Organizing a system of occupational instruction around the teaching of specific competencies has several desirable characteristics. Here are some of them, briefly presented.

It is streamlined and efficient. Using competencies and the instructional techniques which are associated with this method results in one of the most streamlined and efficient ways of imparting knowledge and skills that is known. Competency-based instruction is systematic and goal-oriented. There is little waste in a properly designed and executed system of competency-based instruction. All activity is ideally purposeful and goal directed.

It is a psychologically sound method. The focusing of all activity on a purpose is sometimes referred to as goal-oriented instruction. This is a key feature of an organized system of competency-based instruction. Goals of specific occupational competencies are the takeoff points for a student in the beginning of the learning cycle. Competency-based instruction clearly focuses on the task to be accomplished so it is one of the soundest instructional techniques known.

Ideally, occupational proficiencies are sequenced in a hierarchy of increasing difficulty in a competency-based instruction system. Students generally proceed from mastering the simple tasks at the beginning of the learning cycle to the more complex as their experience and proficiency grows. A student in an automotive mechanics class, for example, would have to master the basic theories associated with internal combustion engines prior to learning how to flush out a fuel line.

We will examine the validity of competency-based instruction systems in the last chapter of this book. It is sufficient to point out in this section that a wealth of information and research related to learning theory confirms that the methods used in competency-based instruction systems promote highly positive and productive learning experiences.

It is accountable. The ultimate test of accountability in an occupational instruction program is whether former students are successfully employed after completing the program. You can increase the number of placements by implementing a competency-based instruction system. A system grounded on precise identification of the occupational skills to be gained provides for built-in accountability.

Use your advisory committee and local employers to assist you in creating, evaluating, and revising your specific job title competencies. The purpose of this cooperation is ultimately to increase the accountability of your program. The closer you can align the skill proficiencies you teach with the needs of local employers, the more accountable the program will become. The students will most certainly be the winners because the more valid you make the curriculum, the more employable your former students will be.

A system of competency instruction can provide another form of accountability for you—an accurate documentation of what you did with your instructional time. A well-developed system of competency-based instruction represents a comprehensive lesson plan in action. Under any set of circumstances you can review the current level of your students' competency attainment and be able to describe in detail what has happened in your program.

It is individualized. One of the biggest failings of traditional classroom instruction has been that virtually the same type of performance has been expected from a widely varied group of students. This is simply impossible to achieve. There is no conceivable way in which all students can become technically competent at the same time, as, for example, in the understanding of logic circuits or in the programming of a computer. Those students who experience difficulty at the beginning of a traditional instruction program will more than likely continue to have problems throughout the course. This is because a poor foundation has been laid prior to an attempt at mastering more complex skills.

For example, a student who does not learn the basic formulas for computing the volume of a gas, electrical theory, and basic fluid mechanics will have difficulty completing a refrigeration course. The value of the student's entire instructional program is undermined if basic skill levels necessary for building a foundation for further learning are not attained.

A system of instruction which focuses on a particular level of skill proficiency as a goal, and which specifically directs each individual student through logical steps designed to develop basic proficiency, has the advantage of making it possible for 15 or 20 students in the same class to be at different levels of achievement. A student can, theoretically, take as long as necessary to master skills for a chosen job title. Students are allowed to proceed at their own rate of learning in a competency-based instruction system. There is never confusion as to where the student is on the progress record of performance, or in what area the student may be experiencing difficulty. The instructor is able to provide extra assistance in a timely fashion.

You might ask, "What are the real costs associated with a competency-based instruction system?" The following section outlines an answer to this basic question.

What Will It Cost to Develop and Use a Competency-Based Instruction System?

The costs that are associated with the development and use of a competency-based instruction system can be categorized into two general areas: dollar cost and time.

One would expect that the dollar cost of implementing a competency-based instruction system would be rather high. This is not necessarily true. Large amounts of money are not required to implement the methods and techniques which are associated with competency skills instruction.

Let's construct an analogy which will serve to increase your understanding of the dollar cost of a competency-based instruction system and its wide-ranging extremes. The actual cost pattern is very much like one you would encounter when outfitting yourself for the game of golf.

You could quite easily spend $3,000 on a golf cart with a built-in refrigerator and radio, or you could carry your own clubs, drink water from the fountain, and walk the 18 holes. Your game of golf would be relatively unaffected, assuming you have the physical strength to carry the clubs and walk the distance of the course. You could purchase or rent a pull-cart for your clubs for a reasonable amount if you chose not to carry your bag.

Clubs, too, could either be bought at a garage sale for a small price, or thousands of dollars could be spent for specially weighted clubs, which could also be plated with precious metal and have your initials affixed to each club. In either case, the quality of your game may not necessarily reflect the dollar cost of your equipment.

Great dollar expense can also be incurred when organizing and implementing a competency-based instruction system. A heavy-duty work station, including a brand new eight-cylinder engine permanently mounted on a stand, could be purchased for an automotive mechanics class. This work station would more than likely come with an operations manual that would give instructions on how to put in "bugs" in order to improve students' trouble-shooting skills. This ready-made work station would have a high price tag.

On the other hand, a salvaged eight-cylinder engine could be obtained at a lower cost (or possibly as a donation from local employers or members of the advisory committee). The engine could then be mounted by someone who had welding expertise and a few feet of angle iron. Once the engine was securely fastened, the project could be completed for the price of a few gauges, some sheet metal, and an ignition switch. You would have created a "live" work station to be used as a controlled learning situation through which your students could develop competencies. An instructor would have to create original ideas for bugging the engine, if the work station was teacher-constructed, but this is relatively simple to accomplish.

The same pattern can be found in virtually every occupational instruction program. Very expensive television trainers can be purchased to serve as work stations for students. Those same expensive work stations can be created by instructors from donated television sets. You may encounter similar cost pattern contrasts when organizing other phases of your competency-based instruction system.

Illustration 7. Carefully organized work stations allow students and instructors to manage their time more efficiently.

When planning your curriculum, it is important to remember that the cost of implementing a competency-based instruction system is divided into two areas. "Time" is the second component of the overall cost of development. Great investments of time, persistence, interest, and dedication are what it takes to organize, implement, and maintain a competency-based instruction system. You should realize that while the dollar cost can vary significantly, there is a minimum investment of time that must be devoted to the development and implementation of a competency-based instruction system. The process of selecting job titles, writing, revising, and validating competencies, and selecting and designing appropriate learning activities could take years. Because competency-based instruction is a vital and dynamic method, it is almost continuously in a state of revision and must be extremely flexible to changes in technology and student achievement.

You can, therefore, expect to invest a goodly portion of time performing the following activities when creating a competency-based instruction system:

- Selecting job titles under which to train students
- Identifying sets of knowledge and skills which must be developed
- Writing competency statements
- Organizing learning activities
- Selecting and developing instructional materials
- Testing and evaluation
- Validating and revising competency statements
- Conducting liaison activities related to curriculum within the employment community

The chapters which follow will focus on various methods which you may use to develop and effectively operate a competency-based instruction system.

REVIEW QUESTIONS

1. What is an occupational competency?
2. What is the main goal of occupational instruction?

3. Describe, in your own words, the meaning of a competency-based instruction system.

4. What are the five main components of a competency-based instruction system?

5. Define the phrase "job title competencies."

6. What is meant by the term "organized learning activity"?

7. Why must learning resources be efficiently managed in a competency-based instruction system?

8. What is the difference between the testing and evaluation of competency achievement?

9. Why is it necessary to maintain an extensive system for the keeping of competency records?

10. List at least three advantages of using a competency-based instruction system.

11. Why is a competency-based instruction system more accountable than a traditional program of instruction?

12. Describe the two categories of cost which are associated with converting to a competency-based instruction system.

CHAPTER

Job Title Identification

TWO

T HE nature of a competency-based instruction system was explored in Chapter 1. The advantages of using this system of instruction, which focuses on the development of marketable skills, were also presented. This chapter is devoted to a discussion of how to select a job title for use in a competency-based instruction system. The proper selection of a job title under which to prepare students for employment is the foundation of such a system. The method which you follow in making a choice of an occupational title is critical to the success of your curriculum conversion.

On completion of this chapter you will be familiar with the techniques and resources that are used to select specific fields of employment for which you can provide appropriate occupational instruction. The employment opportunities for students who complete your revised program of instruction will be greatly increased if you use the methods suggested in this section. The curriculum you design will be especially suited to the unique sets of circumstances faced by you and your students.

Information contained in this chapter will help you to answer the following questions:

What is a job title?
What are the advantages of using job titles?
How do you select an appropriate job title?

What are the occupations for which you can prepare students?

What Is a Job Title?

A job title is a specialized occupational classification which may be a part of a broader field of employment. Examples of several job titles which are included in the field of automotive mechanics are:

> Transmission Specialist
> Brake Mechanic
> Automotive Front-End Mechanic

All of these job titles require both general and specialized knowledge related to automotive mechanics. Any one of these three employment classifications is a job title for which students can be prepared in a well-equipped automotive mechanics program. Job titles are thus narrower and more specialized classifications of what have traditionally been thought of, in occupational instruction programs, as fields of employment.

Another example of how a field of employment can be broken down into specialized job titles, for which occupational instruction can be provided, is illustrated below. The designation meat cutter or butcher is a broad field of employment that has many job titles associated with it. Among them are:

> Meat Trimmer
> Meat Grader
> Meat Dresser
> Final Dressing Cleaner
> Meat Boner

Each of the above-mentioned job titles is related to what is normally described as the employment field of butcher, but they are *specialized* functions of this occupational title.

The labor market in our country indicates a trend toward increased specialization. An example of how specialization and other factors may affect the nature of a job title training program is shown below in the contrast between two commercial fishing training programs in different parts of the nation.

There is a difference between job tasks that a commercial fisherman performs in the Pacific Northwest as compared to those in the Lake Okeechobee region of Florida. The more appropriate job title for a commercial fisherman working on Lake Okeechobee might be "cat-fisherman," because the catfish is the largest commercial fishing crop in that particular region. A host of very specialized baiting and trap-making techniques must be employed by an adept catfisherman to make a living. A commercial fisherman in the Pacific Northwest, on the other hand, might be more appropriately referred to as a "tuna fisherman."

The selection of a job title under which to prepare students should be based primarily on the employment opportunities in your area. This is an important point to remember. The job title which you select must also be in line with the students' employment goals and ideally be descriptive of the tasks which will be carried out on the job.

What Are the Advantages of Using Job Titles?

The greatest advantage in using specific job titles as a basis for the competency-based instruction program in your area is that the curriculum is built on local employment needs. The total instructional effort is therefore streamlined. There may be a core of knowledge to develop which is common to a broad range of occupational fields, but a majority of the instruction in a competency-based system is specifically related to the development of skills which are needed by local employers.

All students who are preparing to work in horticulture, for example, may be required to know the basic life cycles of plants regardless of the climate in their particular location. Horticulture students in southern California would not, however, specialize in cultivating maple trees, a tree which grows in more northern regions.

Another advantage in using job titles as a basis on which to build an occupational curriculum is that a liaison between the instructional program and business and industry is promoted. The nature of the processes which the curriculum writer follows in setting up a valid set of competencies for a job title curriculum promotes the alignment of a training program with the needs of employers. The group which will benefit most from this is your students.

A health occupations instructor might determine, for example, that a majority of the employment opportunities in a particular locale is for nurses' aides in nursing homes. It may also be determined that the nursing homes are willing to pay higher salaries for individuals who are skilled as "geriatric nurses' aides." For the benefit of both the student and employer, the instructor should adjust his program to reflect this training need. The instructor would still have to include basic core knowledge that an entry-level nurse's aide should have, but specialized job title training could also be provided to enhance the employability of students.

Selecting job titles as a base for vocational instruction can also be cost effective. Many occupational programs have been designed to prepare individuals for broad fields of employment and as a result more equipment and supply expenses have been incurred than necessary. There is a tendency to purchase more than is required for an occupational program which is general rather than specific.

Accountability is another advantage of using a job title curriculum. The instructor prepares individuals for employment with a particular job title in mind and on completion of the program the student is either competent as an entry-level employee or is not.

The accountability of an automotive mechanics program, for example, is difficult to evaluate when former students are employed at a local filling station and their primary job task is filling automobile tanks with gasoline. A certain degree of program accountability is clear, however, when a student who completes the job title curriculum of "transmission specialist" is employed by one of the large national transmission firms.

The use of job title curricula is compatible with the philosophy and goals of vocational education. The closer that occupational education reflects actual employment opportunities, the nearer the program is to achieving the basic goals of vocational and technical instruction. We will now examine the factors that should be considered when first selecting a job title as the basis on which to construct a competency-based curriculum.

How Do You Select an Appropriate Job Title?

Major questions must be answered prior to making a job title selection for a competency-based instruction system. One of them is, "What are the specific employment opportunities in your area?" Information useful for selecting job titles can be obtained from each of the following sources:

Labor market statistics
Advisory committee feedback

Local economic development councils
Local employers and community surveys
The *Occupational Outlook Handbook*
The *Dictionary of Occupational Titles*

This information is important in assisting you to analyze and select a job title which accurately represents a chance for the future employment of your students. We will examine the nature of the information which can be obtained from each of them.

Labor Market Statistics. This information is tabulated routinely and available to any citizen who requests it. All state employment security offices maintain detailed sets of information compiled by the U.S. Department of Labor on what are known as Standard Metropolitan Statistical Areas (areas which have a population of 50,000 or more). Most of the available data is based on a matrix used by the Department of Labor which lists 200 industries and more than 400 specific occupations.

States often compile their own separate sets of labor statistics. The addresses for these state agencies are listed at the end of this chapter (pp. 49-52).

Labor market statistics are sometimes compiled by trade and professional associations. If you are fortunate enough to have access to this type of information for the area where your program will be used, it should give even more specific data.

The job titles which the instructor will note as showing promise should satisfy two sets of criteria: does the job title rank high in the total number of annual job openings? and, does the job title rank high among the fastest growing occupations in your area? If a job title is listed as one of the fastest growing and has a high number of annual openings, it can be considered a viable job title for a competency-based curriculum.

Advisory Committee Feedback. Instructors in most occupational programs have advisory committees which are made up of employers and interested citizens from the community. Advisory committees often give invaluable advice on what job titles should be offered to the students and also serve as a valid back-up source of information.

The most productive way to approach an advisory committee is to hold a meeting with the group and present them with the evidence that you have gathered from labor market statistics. The members should be able to make a qualitative judgment of this information.

They should be able to give an accurate insight into the special features of the local labor market and help you to evaluate the appropriateness of the job titles you have selected. They should be asked to submit suggestions of job titles that they feel meet the needs of the employers and the community.

Local Economic Development Councils. Many communities have economic development councils whose main purpose is the promotion of the local economy. Economic development councils concentrate their efforts on the analysis and packaging of local demographics to attract new industry, or assist in the development of industry which is currently located in the community. These associations usually have publications which contain information which you could use to help select appropriate job titles for your competency-based program.

The people who are members of the economic development council may also be interested in speaking with you. They provide industry with information on the local educational system and on sources of qualified employees. Establishing mutually satisfying relationship with an economic development council could help you to develop a system of instruction that would enhance the employment opportunities for your students.

Local Employers and Community Surveys. You must be able to identify the potential employers of your students. If you are in the business of producing a product for consumption (employees for employers), you have to know who your customers are. It is very important to develop a list of potential employers.

You can use the contact you have made with advisory committee members and the local economic development council to assist you in this task. You can also refer to the yellow pages of the telephone directory which lists, by industry or business classification, the addresses of firms which may employ students in the fields for which you are preparing them.

Yet another source of information, which might complement the data collection you have already done, is the Chamber of Commerce. Most Chambers of Commerce maintain extensive listings of their members by industry classification. You may be able to obtain a valuable insight into who the potential employers of your students are by seeking assistance from the Chamber of Commerce.

TECHNICIAN EDUCATION YEARBOOK

Illustration 8. Representatives from the local industrial board and the Chamber of Commerce help this instructor assess employer needs.

Once you have developed a tentative listing of potential employers and job titles, you need to construct a questionnaire for the employers you have identified. This will determine if the job titles for which you propose to offer training represent valid employment opportunities. The survey can also be used to assess specific job tasks or requirements which will help you later in developing a competency-based instruction system. You may also be able to determine employment turnover and possible employment expansion directly from potential employers. This would be more timely and accurate information than that obtained from the federal and state labor departments. An example of an occupational survey format for a marketing and sales program, which can be used to assess opportunity for various job titles, is shown in Illustration 9.

OCCUPATIONAL SURVEY
Retail Sales

I. Please answer the following questions by checking the appropriate space to the right of each item.

	Yes	No
1. Do you employ individuals in your business who work as sales clerks?	_____	_____
2. Do you employ persons who work exclusively as cash register operators?	_____	_____
3. Do you employ people whose sole responsibility is that of a stock clerk?	_____	_____

II. If you answered "yes" to Question #1, please answer the following questions in relation to the job classification of *Sales Clerk*.

4. How many sales clerks do you currently employ? _____

5. What is the employee turnover rate per year for sales clerks? _____

6. Do you anticipate an increase in the number of employees that you hire to work in this job classification? _____

7. Do you require previous experience or training of an individual that you would employ? Please explain.

8. Would you be willing to respond to a follow-up survey which would help us determine the specific tasks performed by sales clerks in our community? _____

III. If you answered "yes" to Question #2, please answer the following questions in relation to the job classification of *Cash Register Operator.*

9. How many cash register operators do you currently employ?

_____

10. What is the employee turnover rate per year for cash register operators? _____

11. Do you anticipate an increase in the number of employees that you hire to work in this job classification? _____

12. Do you require previous experience or training of an individual that you would employ as a cash register operator? Please explain.

13. Would you be willing to respond to a follow-up survey which would help us determine the specific tasks performed by cash register operators in our community? _____

IV. If you answered "yes" to Question #3, please answer the following questions in relation to the job classification of *Stock Clerk.*

14. How many stock clerks do you currently employ? _____

15. What is the employee turnover rate per year for stock clerks?

_____

16. Do you anticipate an increase in the number of employees that you hire to work as stock clerks? _____

17. Do you require previous experience or training of an individual that you would employ as a stock clerk? Please explain.

18. Would you be willing to respond to a follow-up survey which would help us determine the specific tasks performed by stock clerks? _____

Illustration 9. Occupational Survey

The *Occupational Outlook Handbook.* This document is published by the federal Department of Labor, Bureau of Labor Statistics. This book may be purchased for a nominal fee from the Superintendent of Documents, U.S. Government Printing Office, Washington, D.C. 20402. The *Handbook* is a primary source of information which will help you to select and verify the most appropriate job titles under which to prepare students for employment. It offers descriptions of what workers in various employment classifications do on the job and the type of preparation or education that is normally required to secure such employment. The *Handbook* also offers projections as to the availability of those jobs in the future.

Each occupation is carefully described in the *Handbook* and is followed by several standard subsections. The information provided is especially useful to an instructor in the process of structuring a competency-based curriculum. Each general description of an occupation is followed by the subsections listed below:

Working Conditions
Places of Employment
Training, Other Qualifications, and Advancement
Employment Outlook
Earnings
Related Occupations
Sources for Additional Information

The *Dictionary of Occupational Titles.* The *DOT* is another resource which can assist you in the selection of a job title. *DOT* is a publication of the U.S. Department of Labor, Employment and Training Administration, and is also available from the U.S. Government Printing Office.

The core of the *DOT* is a detailed description of job titles which have been verified by on-site analyses. Over 75,000 specific occupational titles are included. The *DOT* uses a multi-digit numerical code and a written description to classify and define the various occupational titles. The information contained in the *DOT* is broken down into six basic parts. They are:

The Occupational Code Number
The Occupational Title
The Industry Designation
The Alternate Title (if any)

The Body of the Definition
  a) the lead statement
  b) the task element statements
  c) "may items" (tasks that those in the occupation *may* be required to perform)
Undefined Related Titles (if any)

The *Dictionary* is basically a listing of occupational titles with task descriptions. This resource not only can help the instructor select an appropriate job title for which to prepare individuals for employment, but it can be invaluable in outlining the basic knowledge and skills to be developed by students.

Now that you have created a pool of job titles that may be appropriate to your program, the next step is to determine which of the possible choices can be implemented most effectively. An examination of the elements which must be considered when making your evaluation follows.

What Are the Occupations for Which You Can Prepare Students?

This question requires careful analysis by the instructor developing a competency-based curriculum. Full consideration must be given to all phases of the program prior to making the final selection of a job title. These considerations include:

Personnel qualifications
The adequacy of your training facility
Your equipment and fiscal resources

Personnel qualifications. You will discover a number of job titles under which employment opportunities exist for your students, but you must ask yourself the following question: "For which of the job titles am I (or members of my staff) qualified to prepare students for employment?"

You would be doing your students a disservice if you were inaccurate in your answer and proceeded to design a curriculum for a job title which you are not qualified to teach. First, the development of a competency-based instruction system requires a detailed analysis of job requirements. Also, you could not do a thorough job of curriculum design if your occupational experience and knowledge in the field were limited, because it would be difficult to assess exactly what

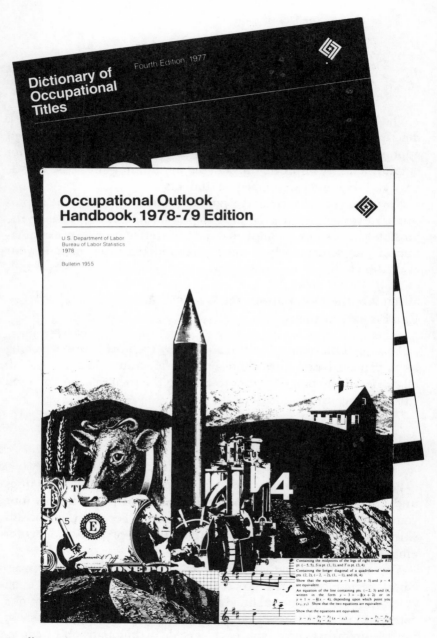

Illustration 10. The *Dictionary of Occupational Titles* and the *Occupational Outlook Handbook* provide invaluable information about jobs and job titles.

the student needs to learn.

The results would be disastrous if an instructor selected a job title under which to prepare students and then was unable to provide quality instruction. You should select only those job titles in which you are confident of your own experience and abilities. Resolve to get further work experience and become updated in the area if you are not totally proficient. Consider the following example.

An instructor who graduated from a general business education program which concentrated on the development of a basic business knowledge (accounting, consumer economics, business law, etc.) should be limited to teaching those skills associated with basic business knowledge. This individual would not be qualified to effectively teach business education skill courses such as shorthand and typing. Even though job titles of secretary and legal secretary represent existing employment opportunities, an instructor should not begin these job title programs without possessing shorthand and typing skills.

Be certain of your own background and capabilities before choosing a job title for your program. Analyze your own qualifications in light of the employment opportunities that exist for your students. Select a job title which you are fully trained for and capable of teaching effectively.

The adequacy of your training facility. You should examine the nature of the job titles for which you have determined that employment opportunities exist and ask yourself the question: "Is my training facility adequate to conduct this type of job training?" The determination of adequacy must include space, safety considerations, and the equipment that will be needed in the instruction program.

The nature of the work performed by the all-around machinist, for example, dictates that certain competencies must be developed in the following areas: chipping, filing, hand tapping, dowel fitting, riveting, and the operation of various specialized machine tools. There must be provisions for blueprint reading in the classroom, as well as for some mechanical drawing.

There must also be sufficient space in which to perform all of the functions required under an entry-level job title. There is no real purpose in converting a high school metalworking class, for example, into a job title training program for preparing all-around machinists if there is literally no room in which to install and operate specialized machine tools safely. Facility considerations are so vital that they often set the limits of what can be accomplished in an occupational training program. An instructor cannot prepare individuals to become photographic developers, for instance, if the facilities do not include a light-tight darkroom.

Prior to making a final decision, the instructor should review training space requirements for a job title by using professional literature, catalogs, and pamphlets. Visiting local employers can also lend an insight into the physical space requirements needed to prepare individuals for a specific job title employment.

Your equipment and fiscal resources. You may already have the necessary equipment and supplies in your classroom/laboratory or may have to secure them through donations or purchases. Before making your decision, you should make a full inventory of the equipment that you have which could be converted for use in the job title programs you are considering implementing. Once this is done, you can compare current training resources with what you will actually need to provide for quality competency-based instruction.

You must have the resources, including adequate funding, to make up the difference between what you have and what you will need. Remember, however, that it is possible to begin a program with resources that are somewhat less than what you ideally would like to have.

The example from Chapter 1 of the individual who wishes to begin playing golf made the point that there is a broad range of initial expense that could be incurred. Golf can be played with a ball and one club or with a full set of expensive equipment. You could become proficient, however, in the basics of golf and probably record a respectable score with only a minimal amount of equipment. The same pattern can hold true in an occupational training program. You must, in any case, have the essential "tools of the trade" available with which to develop competencies and a place in which you can safely apply them. The fiscal resources that are allocated to occupational training programs are often far from desirable, but with advisory committee assistance and help from the business community your basic training needs can often be met.

As we have seen, the process of selecting a job title is deliberate and systematic. The following example is a step-by-step illustration of how a job title might be selected employing the suggestions which were introduced in this chapter.

Illustration II. The facilities for this carpentry program provide adequate space and equipment for the development of a variety of job-related skills.

DEVELOPMENTAL EXAMPLE: Part 1
Choosing a Job Title

Assume that you are the new instructor in a carpentry program at a comprehensive high school. In past years the number of students enrolled in the program has been twenty. You have made a tentative examination of the circumstances and cannot find any evidence of these students' having been employed as a direct result of completing the course. You have also discovered that there is a strong apprenticeship program in the area for carpenters. You believe, nonetheless, that you can use your facility to prepare individuals for employment opportunities which may exist in this field. Assume, also, that you will be converting the curriculum to one that is competency based. Your first task would be to review the past course descriptions and outlines to determine what the history of the course has been. The traditional course description and outline for a carpentry program is shown in Illustration 12.

CARPENTRY: Course Description [traditional]

Construction, installation, and repair of structures of wood, plywood, and wallboard using carpenters' tools. Blueprint reading, lumber selection, layout, fastening, and assembly of various structures. A *Certificate of Achievement* is awarded for successful course completion.

Occupational Definition: Constructs, erects, installs, and repairs structures and fixtures of wood, plywood, and wallboard, using carpenters' hand and power tools while conforming to local building codes. Studies blueprints, sketches, or building plans for information pertaining to type of material required and dimensions of the structure to be fabricated. Prepares layout, using rule, framing squares, and calipers. Marks cutting and assembly lines on materials, using pencil, chalk, and marking gages. Shapes materials to prescribed measurements, using saws, chisels, and planes. Assembles cut and shaped materials and fastens them together with nails, dowel pins, or glue. Verifies trueness of structures. Erects framework for structures and lays subflooring. Builds stairs. Lays out and installs partitions. Fits and installs windows, doors, door frames, and weather stripping, performs interior and exterior trim and finish work. Constructs forms and chutes.

Job Possibilities: Layout Carpenter, Finish Carpenter, House Carpenter, Door Hanger, Stair Builder, Trim Setter, Carpenter Apprentice, Joiner, etc.

Course Outline

I. **Hand and power tools**
   A. Types of hand tools
      1. Safe use of hand tools
      2. Measuring devices
      3. Saws
      4. Care of hand tools
   B. Types of power tools
      1. Safe use of power tools
      2. Electric drill
      3. Saber saw
      4. Reciprocating saw
      5. Electric plane
      6. Router
      7. Belt and disc sanders
      8. Radial arm saw
      9. Table saw
II. **Transits and levels**
   A. The builder's level
   B. The transit level
   C. Plumbing
III. **The framing square**
   A. Scales and tables

1. Glossary of terms
2. Hundredth scale
3. Octagon scale
4. Essex board measure
5. Brace measure

IV. **Construction fasteners**
   A. Nail identification
   B. Screw identification
   C. Bolts
   D. Framing anchors
V. **Building materials**
   A. Wood
      1. Physical properties of wood
      2. Wood identification
      3. Lumber sizes
      4. Board measure
   B. Plywood: types and use
   C. Particleboard
   D. Hardboard
   E. Adhesives
VI. **Foundations**

A. Architectural symbols
B. Plot layout
C. Excavation requirements
D. Footings
E. Foundation walls
F. Slab construction
G. Steps
H. Walks and driveways

VII. **Floor framing**
A. Girders
B. Wood posts
C. Steel posts
D. Joists
E. Double joists
F. Bridging
G. Subflooring types

VIII. **Wall framing**
A. Balloon framing
B. Platform framing
C. Wall frame members
   1. Sole plate
   2. Studs
   3. Top plate
   4. Bracing
   5. Corner posts
Wall framing
E. Framing for openings
F. Ceiling joists

IX. **Roof framing**
A. Types of roofs
   1. Flat
   2. Shed
   3. Gable
   4. Hip
   5. Gambrel
B. Roof framing members
   1. Common rafters
   2. Hip rafters
   3. Valley rafters
   4. Jack rafters
   5. Hip jacks
   6. Valley jacks
   7. Cripple jacks
C. Layout for common rafters
D. Erecting roofs
   1. Gable
   2. Hip

E. Roof sheathing

X. **Finish roofing**
A. Deck preparation
B. Roofing underlayment
C. Flashing
D. Asphalt shingles
E. Rolls roofing
F. Wood shingles
G. Wood shakes
H. Other types

XI. **Windows**
A. Types of windows
   1. Double hung
   2. Casement windows
   3. Sliding windows
   4. Awning windows
   5. Bow and bay windows
   6. Jalousies
B. Installation of windows

XII. **Doors and frames**
A. Exterior wood doors
B. Sliding glass doors
C. Garage doors and frames
D. Interior doors

XIII. **Exterior wall coverings**
A. Horizontal siding
B. Vertical siding
C. Wood shingles and shakes
D. Mineral siding fiber
E. Hardboard siding
F. Asphalt sidings
G. Aluminum siding
H. Vinyl siding
I. Stucco
J. Veneer

XIV. **Stair construction**
A. Types of stairs
B. Stair landings
C. Stairwell rough framing
D. Ratio of rise to tread
E. Stringers and carriages

XV. **Interior wall finish**
A. Plaster
B. Gypsum drywall
C. Masonry walls
D. Paneling

Illustration 12. Traditional course description and outline for a carpentry program.

The preceding course description and outline are quite comprehensive in their scope. The detailed nature of the course, as it currently exists, may very well prevent the instructor from effectively preparing a student for employment during the typical school year.

The section of the course description entitled "Job Possibilities" implies that a student completing this course could be employed in a wide variety of jobs after taking this course. Most instructors familiar with the field of carpentry and with the labor market know that for individuals to become employable in all of these areas would be nearly impossible.

The task that confronts the carpentry instructor in our "Developmental Example" is to select the job title or titles for which employment opportunities exist in the community. The steps that this instructor may follow in selecting a job title for students prior to converting the curriculum to a competency-based system follow.

1. *Examine the* Dictionary of Occupational Titles. The *Dictionary of Occupational Titles* lists the major employment classifications which are related to carpentry. By referring to the *DOT* the instructor would be able to choose from the wide range of titles which are identified. The *DOT* lists the following job titles and codes which are related to carpentry:

860.131-010	SUPERVISOR, ACOUSTICAL TILE CARPENTER
860.131-014	SUPERVISOR, BOATBUILDERS, WOOD
860.131-018	SUPERVISOR, CARPENTERS
860.131-022	SUPERVISOR, JOINERS
860.131-026	SUPERVISOR, MOLD CONSTRUCTION
860.131-010	CARPENTER-LABOR SUPERVISOR
860.261-010	CARPENTER INSPECTOR
860.281-010	CARPENTER, MAINTENANCE
860.281-014	CARPENTER, SHIP
860.381-010	ACOUSTICAL CARPENTER
860.381-014	BOATBUILDER APPRENTICE, WOOD
860.381-018	BOATBUILDER, WOOD
860.381-022	CARPENTER (construction)
860.381-026	CARPENTER APPRENTICE
860.381-020	CARPENTER, BRIDGE
860.381-034	CARPENTER, MOLD
860.381-038	CARPENTER, RAILCAR
860.381-042	CARPENTER, ROUGH
860.381-046	FORM BUILDER
860.381-050	JOINER
860.381-054	JOINER APPRENTICE
860.381-058	SHIPWRIGHT
860.381-062	SHIPWRIGHT, APPRENTICE

860.381-066   TANK BUILDER AND ERECTOR
860.381-070   TANK ERECTOR
860.664-010   CARPENTER (manufactured buildings)
860.664-014   JOINER HELPER
860.664-018   SHIPWRIGHT HELPER
860.681-010   CARPENTER (manufactured buildings) II
860.684-010   BUILDER, BEAM (manufactured buildings)
860.684-014   SIDER (manufactured buildings)

2. *Review the data contained in the* Occupational Outlook Handbook. The instructor should also locate the section of the *Occupational Outlook Handbook* which relates to carpentry. The *Handbook* analyzes the nature of the work encountered in the occupational field and examines the outlook for employment. The instructor who is choosing a job title or titles as a basis for a competency-based instruction system can find additional information in the *Handbook* that is invaluable in the process of selection.

For example, the description for carpentry in the *Handbook* covers the scope of work performed by carpenters and points out that there is a degree of specialization within the field. This factor should provide a clue for the instructor in our example that specialized carpentry-related employment opportunities may exist in the community. The *Handbook* also points out that carpentry is broadly categorized into two groups: rough carpentry and finish carpentry. This information by itself is essential to the instructor when selecting viable job titles under which to prepare individuals for employment.

Other useful information in the *Handbook* which assists the instructor in the search for a job title and in building a competency-based curriculum includes:

Working Conditions
Places of Employment
Training, Other Qualifications, and Advancement
Employment Outlook
Earnings
Related Occupations
Sources for Additional Information

3. *Examine the local labor market statistics.* Local labor market data should inform the instructor what job titles have the highest number of annual openings and which job titles are among the fastest growing in the area.

Let's assume, for the purpose of our example, that the following job titles related to carpentry meet the criteria outlined above:

Carpenter
Boatbuilder, wood
Rough carpenter
Maintenance carpenter

The instructor is now able to narrow the list of job titles selected from the *DOT* to those which may represent employment opportunities in the community. Further analysis can now take place.

4. *Contact the Chamber of Commerce and local trade associations.* The Chamber of Commerce and trade associations (e.g., the Contractors' Association) may provide the instructor with a list of the employers who hire carpenters in the local area. They may also be able to comment authoritatively on the list of job titles which the instructor has chosen for consideration. The list of job titles could possibly be reduced further by consulting Chamber of Commerce and trade association data, but generally the instructor will proceed to the next step in the job title selection process without major alteration to the initial list.

5. *Conduct a community survey of employers.* The purpose of the community survey should be to ask potential employers directly if there is a need to employ individuals under the job titles which have been selected and, if so, what the average number of annual openings is. An example of an employment survey was presented earlier in Illustration 9.

Let's assume that the instructor in the "Developmental Example" prepares an employment survey for the four job titles which were identified as having the greatest potential in the local labor market. The survey would then be mailed to the employers who were identified by the Chamber of Commerce and by the Contractors' Association. Assume that the following employment information was obtained for each job title on the tentative list:

CARPENTER: Individuals employed under this job title generally are either apprentices or journeymen. Most employers do not feel that they can obtain qualified carpenters from other sources.

BOATBUILDER, WOOD: There are fewer than 3 job openings per year in this job title although there are a number of employers.

ROUGH CARPENTER: There are more than 80 job openings annually which are documented for rough carpenters. The employers surveyed indicate that about two-thirds of the openings are for apprentices or journeymen carpenters.

MAINTENANCE CARPENTER: There are at least 20 annual job openings in the area of maintenance carpentry. Most of the individuals who are employed in this job title work in large apartment dwellings.

The data that has been gathered by the instructor in our example would indicate that there are employment opportunities for rough carpenters and maintenance carpenters. Both job titles require general knowledge and skills related to carpentry, and the job title of maintenance carpenter requires more refined carpentry skills and knowledge. The instructor must now ask the advisory committee what job title students should be prepared for.

6. *Use advisory committee feedback.* We will assume for the purpose of the "Developmental Example" that the instructor has selected an advisory committee which is representative of the employment community. The advisory committee would more than likely recommend that the instructor use the job title of rough carpenter in the program, because this field had the largest number of possible job openings.

The advisory committee members probably would recommend that two other alternatives be considered. Approach the local apprenticeship program's administrators and determine if they might be willing to accept graduates from the carpentry program as second-year apprentices in their program, or explore the possibility of a job title program for maintenance carpenter which enrolls advanced students.

Before being totally confident in the selection of one or both of these job titles, the instructor must answer the remaining questions which were suggested earlier in this chapter:

1. Are you qualified to train rough carpenters and maintenance carpenters?

2. Do you have the necessary physical facilities in which to prepare rough carpenters and maintenance carpenters?

3. Do you have the necessary equipment and fiscal resources which are required to prepare rough carpenters and maintenance carpenters?

The advisory committee can help our instructor to answer the second and third questions by examining the resources at hand. The instructor, however, is the only one who can answer the first question.

Instructors should not attempt to prepare students for a job title if they are not capable of providing quality instruction. The potential students for a job title program of this type might be better served if the instructor persuaded the school's administration to allow the teaching of a woodworking course. The instructor could then gain the knowledge and experience necessary to prepare students under either or both of these job titles in the summer or through part-time employment. An instructor is well on the way to developing a sound competency-based instruction system, which will assist students in earning a livelihood, if the answer to all of the questions on p. 47 is "Yes!"

REVIEW QUESTIONS

1. What is meant by the term *job title*?

2. Select a broad occupational field. List a number of job titles which might exist within the employment classification.

3. List at least three advantages of using job titles as a basis for occupational instruction.

4. Describe, in your own words, how each of the following resources can be used to assist in the selection of a job title under which to prepare students for employment:

    a. Labor market statistics
    b. Advisory committees
    c. Local economic development councils
    d. Local employers
    e. Occupational surveys
    f. The *Occupational Outlook Handbook*
    g. The *Dictionary of Occupational Titles*

5. What type of information should you attempt to obtain from an occupational survey?

6. Explain how your own background and experience can influence the selection of a job title under which to prepare students for employment.

7. Assume that you are the new instructor in a vocational program and you wish to select a job title. Explain, in your own words, the steps you would follow in selecting a job title.

SOURCES OF STATE LABOR MARKET STATISTICS

Alabama

Chief, Research and Statistics
Department of Industrial Relations
Industrial Relations Bldg.
649 Monroe St.
Montgomery, Alabama 36160

Alaska

Chief, Research and Analysis
Employment Security Division
Department of Labor
P.O. Box 3-7000
Juneau, Alaska 99811

Arizona

Manager, Labor Market Research
and Analysis
Department of Economic Security
P.O. Box 6123
Phoenix, Arizona 85005

Arkansas

Chief, Research and Statistics
Employment Security Division
P.O. Box 2981
Little Rock, Arkansas 72203

California

Chief, Employment Data and
Research Division
Employment Development
Department
800 Capitol Mall
Sacramento, California 95814

Colorado

Chief, Research and Analysis
Division of Employment
Department of Labor and
Employment
251 East 12th Ave.
Denver, Colorado 80203

Connecticut

Director, Research and Information
Connecticut Employment Security
Division
200 Folly Brook Blvd.
Weatherfield, Connecticut 06109

Delaware

Chief, Office of Research, Planning
and Evaluation
Department of Labor
801 West 14th St.
Wilmington, Delaware 19899

District of Columbia

Chief, Division of Manpower
Reports and Analysis
Office of Administration
and Management Services
D.C. Department of Manpower
605 G St. NW
Washington, D.C. 20001

Florida

Director, Research and Statistics
Division of Employment Security
Florida Department of Commerce
1720 South Gadsden St.
Tallahassee, Florida 32304

Georgia

Director, Information Systems
Employment Security Agency
Department of Labor
254 Washington St. SW
Atlanta, Georgia 30334

Hawaii

Chief, Research and Statistics
Department of Labor and Industrial
Relations
825 Mililani St.
Honolulu, Hawaii 96813

Idaho

Chief, Research and Analysis
Department of Employment
P.O. Box 35
Boise, Idaho 83707

Illinois

Manager, Research and Analysis
    Division
Bureau of Employment Security
Department of Labor
910 South Michigan Ave.
Chicago, Illinois 60605

Indiana

Chief of Research
    Employment Security Division
10 North Senate Ave.
Indianapolis, Indiana 46204

Iowa

Chief, Research and Statistics
Employment Security Commission
1000 East Grand Ave.
Des Moines, Iowa 50319

Kansas

Chief, Research and Analysis
    Department
Employment Security Division
Department of Labor
401 Topeka Ave.
Topeka, Kansas 66603

Kentucky

Director, Research and Special
    Projects
Department of Human Resources
State Office Building Annex
Frankfort, Kentucky 40601

Louisiana

Chief, Research and Statistics
Department of Employment Security
P.O. Box 44094
Baton Rouge, Louisiana 70804

Maine

Director, Manpower Research
    Division
Employment Security Commission
20 Union St.
Augusta, Maine 04330

Maryland

Director, Research and Analysis
Department of Human Resources
1400 Eutaw St.
Baltimore, Maryland 21201

Massachusetts

Director, Research and Statistics
    Division
Division of Employment Security
Hurley Bldg.
Government Center
Boston, Massachusetts 02114

Michigan

Director, Research and Statistics
    Division
Employment Security Commission
Department of Labor Bldg.
7310 Woodward Ave.
Detroit, Michigan 48202

Minnesota

Director, Research and Planning
Department of Employment
    Services
390 North Robert St.
St. Paul, Minnesota 55101

Mississippi

Chief, Research and Statistics
Employment Security Commission
P.O. Box 1699
Jackson, Mississippi 39205

Missouri

Chief, Research and Analysis
Division of Employment Security
Department of Labor and
    Industrial Relations
P.O. Box 59
Jefferson City, Missouri 65101

Montana

Chief, Research and Analysis
Employment Security Division
P.O. Box 1728
Helena, Montana 59601

Nebraska

Chief, Research and Statistics
Division of Employment
Department of Labor
P.O. Box 94600
State House Station
Lincoln, Nebraska 68509

Nevada

Chief, Manpower Information
    and Research
Employment Security Department
500 East Third St.
Carson City, Nevada 89701

New Hampshire

Supervisor, Economic Analysis
    and Reports
Department of Employment
    Security
32 South Main St.
Concord, New Hampshire 03301

New Jersey

Director, Division of Planning
    and Research
Department of Labor and Industry
John Fitch Plaza
Trenton, New Jersey 08625

New Mexico

Chief, Research and Statistics
Employment Security Commission
P.O. Box 1928
Albuquerque, New Mexico 87103

New York

Director, Division of Research
    and Statistics
Department of Labor
2 World Trade Center
New York, New York 10047

North Carolina

Manager, Bureau of Employment
    Security Research
Employment Security Commission
P.O. Box 25903
Raleigh, North Carolina 27602

North Dakota

Chief, Reports and Analysis
Employment Security Bureau
P.O. Box 1537
Bismarck, North Dakota 58501

Ohio

Director, Division of Research
    and Statistics
Bureau of Employment Services
145 South Front St.
Columbus, Ohio 43216

Oklahoma

Chief, Research and Planning
    Division
Employment Security Commission
Will Rogers Memorial Office Bldg.
Oklahoma City, Oklahoma 73105

Oregon

Chief, Research and Statistics
Employment Division
875 Union St. NE
Salem, Oregon 97310

Pennsylvania

Director, Research and Statistics
Bureau of Employment Security
Department of Labor and Industry
7th and Forster Sts.
Harrisburg, Pennsylvania 17121

Puerto Rico

Chief of Research and Statistics
Bureau of Employment Security
427 Barbosa Ave.
Hato Rey, Puerto Rico 00917

Rhode Island

Supervisor, Employment Security
     Research
Department of Employment Security
24 Mason St.
Providence, Rhode Island 02903

South Carolina

Director, Manpower Research
     and Analysis
Employment Security Commission
1550 Gadsden St.
Columbia, South Carolina 29202

South Dakota

Chief, Research and Statistics
Employment Security Department
607 North Fourth St.
Box 730
Aberdeen, South Dakota 57401

Tennessee

Chief, Research and Statistics
Department of Employment Security
519 Cordell Hull Bldg.
Nashville, Tennessee 37219

Texas

Chief, Manpower Data Analysis
     and Research
Texas Employment Commission
TEC Bldg.
15th and Congress Ave.
Austin, Texas 78778

Utah

Director, Reports and Analysis
Department of Employment Security
P.O. Box 11249
Salt Lake City, Utah 84111

Vermont

Chief, Research and Statistics
Department of Employment Security
P.O. Box 488
Montpelier, Vermont 05602

Virginia

Chief, Manpower Research
Virginia Employment Commission
P.O. Box 1358
Richmond, Virginia 23211

Washington

Chief, Research and Statistics
Employment Security Department
P.O. Box 367
Olympia, Washington 98504

West Virginia

Chief, Research and Statistics
Department of Employment Security
112 California Ave.
Charleston, West Virginia 25305

Wisconsin

Director, Research and Statistics
Department of Industry, Labor
     and Human Relations
P.O. Box 2209
Madison, Wisconsin 53701

Wyoming

Chief, Research and Analysis
Employment Security Commission
P.O. Box 2760
Casper, Wyoming 82601

Listing
Broad Clusters
of Skills
and Knowledge

THE advantages of using competencies as the basis for a teaching strategy and the process to be followed in selecting a job title were outlined in the preceding chapters. The analysis procedure for selecting a job title included a step-by-step assessment of available employment data and a survey of local employers. All possible program limitations were evaluated and after careful consideration an appropriate job title, for which a competency-based curriculum will be designed, was chosen. The next sequence of activities used in developing a competency-based instruction system identifies the competencies that are required to obtain entry-level employment under the job title that has been selected. An example follows of the broad sets of knowledge and skills which may be required for competency in a given job title.

How Do You Identify Broad Sets
of Skills and Knowledge?

We have chosen the job title of bricklayer as an example. Illustration 13 lists the clusters of skills and knowledge associated with this occupational title. This illustration should help clarify the nature of the curriculum writer's task when developing this type of listing for a chosen job title. This listing represents the primary job tasks that the bricklayer must perform. An outline of this type is what the instructor who is developing a competency-based curriculum must produce. It provides the foundation for developing the entire competency-based instruction system.

BRICKLAYER: Job Skill Requirements

1. The ability to lay the following types of building materials:
   a. brick
   b. structural tile
   c. concrete cinderblock
   d. glass block
   e. gypsum
   f. terra-cotta block
2. The ability to construct the following types of masonry structures:
   a. walls
   b. partitions
   c. arches
3. The ability to measure distances accurately from specified reference points.
4. The ability to mark lines on a working surface and to lay out work.
5. The ability to use a trowel properly.
6. The skill to lay a bed of mortar to serve as a base and binder for block.
7. The skill to apply mortar properly to the end of a block and to position it in the mortar bed.
8. The ability to align, level, and embed block in mortar, allowing for a specified thickness of joint.
9. The skill to finish mortar properly between bricks using a point tool or trowel.
10. The skill to break bricks to fit spaces too small for the whole brick, using the edge of a trowel or brick hammer.
11. The ability to determine vertical and horizontal alignment of courses, using a plumb bob, gaugeline, and level.

Illustration 13. Broad sets of skills and knowledge for the job title of bricklayer.

There are a variety of ways to identify the sets of proficiencies that employers desire of a person employed under a particular job title. Some of the methods are:

1. Use the *Dictionary of Occupational Titles*
2. Refer to state curriculum guides
3. Examine textbooks
4. Use manufacturers' handbooks or technical manuals
5. Get help from trade associations and unions
6. Draw on personal expertise
7. Consult your advisory committee

At this point let's return to the "Developmental Example" used in Chapter 2. Assume that the instructor has settled on rough carpenter as the job title under which to prepare students, and examine how each of the suggested procedures helps in formulating a list of the broad sets of skills and knowledge required for this job.

DEVELOPMENTAL EXAMPLE: Part 2
Identifying Broad Sets of Skills and Knowledge

1. *Use the* Dictionary of Occupational Titles. You will recall that in Chapter 2 the *Dictionary of Occupational Titles* helped the instructor select a job title under which to prepare students for employment. The *DOT* is also an invaluable tool for use in identifying the broad sets of proficiencies which are required under a job title. The *DOT*, as mentioned earlier, is published by the U.S. Department of Labor, Employment and Training Administration. Copies can be obtained for a small fee from the Superintendent of Documents, U.S. Government Printing Office, Washington, DC 20402.

The *DOT* contains complete descriptions of job tasks and duties for more than 20,000 occupational titles. One of the most useful features of the *DOT*, for individuals who are involved in curriculum development in vocational education, is the section of the publication which lists job requirements. The job requirements are written in descriptive form under each job title. Let's examine a typical listing and its accompanying description:

604.685-026 LATHE OPERATOR, PRODUCTION (machine shop) automatic-
lathe operator; engine-lathe operator, production; turret-lathe
operator, production.

Tends one or more previously setup lathes, such as turret lathes, *engine lathes*, and chucking machines, to perform one of a series of repetitive operations, such as turning, boring, threading, or facing of metal workpieces according to specifications on production basis: Lifts workpiece manually or with hoist, and positions and secures it between lathe centers, in chuck or in holding *fixture*, using wrench, or places it in automatic loading mechanism. Starts machine and turns handwheels to feed tools to workpiece or engages automatic feed. Observes machining operation to detect malfunction or excessive tool wear. Verifies conformance of machined work to specifications, using fixed gauges, calipers, and micrometers. Changes worn tools, using wrenches. May machine plastics or other nonmetallic materials. May be designated by type of machine tended or operation performed such as KNURLING MACHINE OPERATOR (pen & pencil); TAPPER (clock and watch)I.

Using the *DOT*, the curriculum writer can compile a listing of knowledge and skills for a job title by inferring and extracting information which is contained in the description. We will now demonstrate, using the example of rough carpenter, how the *Dictionary of Occupational Titles* can be useful in the conversion of a curriculum to one that is competency based.

This particular occupational title is coded as **860.381-042** in the *DOT.* The description of this job title is as follows:

860.381-042 CARPENTER, ROUGH (constr.) bracer.
Builds rough wooden structures, such as concrete forms, scaffolds, tunnel and sewer supports, and temporary frame shelters, according to sketches, blueprints, or oral instructions: Examines specifications to determine dimensions of structure. Measures boards, timbers, or plywood, using square, measuring tape, and ruler, and marks cutting lines on materials, using pencil and scriber. Saws boards and plywood panels to required sizes. Nails cleats (braces) across boards to construct concrete-supporting forms. Braces forms in place with timbers, tie rods, and anchor bolts, for use in building concrete piers, footings, and walls. Erects chutes for pouring concrete. Cuts and assembles timbers to build trestles and cofferdams. Builds falsework to temporarily strengthen, protect, or disguise buildings undergoing construction. Erects scaffolding for buildings and ship structures and installs ladders, handrails, walkways, platforms, and gangways. Installs door and window bucks (rough frames in which finished frames are inserted) in designated positions in building framework, and braces them with boards nailed to framework. Installs subflooring in buildings. Nails plaster grounds (wood or metal strips) to studding to provide guide for PLASTERER (const.). Fits and nails sheathing (first covering of boards) on outer walls and of buildings. Builds sleds from logs and timbers for use in hauling camp buildings and machinery through wooded areas.

At this point in the development of a competency-based curriculum the instructor should carefully analyze the *DOT* description. Sets of knowledge and skills which *might* apply to the duties and responsibilities of a rough carpenter in the community must be identified.

Examining the first few lines of the description for rough carpenter will illustrate how clusters of skills and knowledge might be determined.

> Builds rough wooden structures, such as concrete forms, scaffolds, tunnel and sewer supports, and temporary frame shelters, according to sketches, blueprints, or oral instructions: Examines specifications to determine dimensions of structure. Measures boards, timbers, or plywood, using square, measuring tape, and ruler, and marks cutting lines on materials, using pencil and scriber. Saws boards and plywood panels to required sizes.

By examining these first few sentences, the carpentry instructor in our example should be able to discern many competencies which must be taught to students who are preparing to become rough carpenters.

Read items one through five in the list of knowledge and skills which follows and then reread the first sentence from the *DOT* description which is given above. The first sentence states that the rough carpenter interprets blueprints and sketches and builds concrete forms, scaffolding, tunnel and sewer supports, and temporary frame shelters. Each of these tasks should be stated as a cluster of skill and knowledge. It is important to the process of developing a competency-based instruction system that each cluster of proficiencies be identified in this manner.

Study the remainder of the list of skills and knowledge that was inferred from the first few sentences of the description:

1. The ability to construct basic forms for the pouring of concrete.
2. The ability to construct scaffolds.
3. The ability to construct tunnel and sewer supports.
4. The ability to construct temporary frame shelters.
5. The ability to use portable power tools.
6. The ability to interpret blueprints.
7. The ability to make precision measurements and cuts.
8. The ability to use a steel tape measure.
9. The ability to use a framing square.
10. The ability and knowledge to determine accurately the dimensions of a structure.

The list of the clusters of knowledge and skills should be exhaustive. The 10 clusters which are listed above were synthesized from just a few sentences in the *DOT* description for the job title of rough carpenter. Since a careful listing of all of the competencies that a student must possess to be employable is central to a competency-based instruction system, the instructor who is converting to such a system should continue to compile a list of skills and knowledge from the *DOT* description in this manner until the full text has been examined.

Examine the next few sentences of the job description which was taken from the *DOT*:

> Nails cleats (braces) across boards to construct concrete-supporting forms. Braces forms in place with timbers, tie rods, and anchor bolts, for use in building concrete piers, footings, and walls. Erects chutes for pouring concrete.

The following proficiencies are taken from this section of the *DOT* description:

11. The ability to fasten wooden structures together properly.
12. The knowledge to select proper fasteners for various jobs.
13. The ability and skill to properly brace concrete forms using lumber.
14. The ability and skill to brace forms using tie rods and anchor bolts.
15. The knowledge and skill to form concrete piers of varying dimensions.
16. The knowledge and skill to form footings of varying dimensions.
17. The knowledge and skill to form walls of varying dimensions.
18. The ability to construct chutes properly for the pouring of concrete.

Repetitive wording is often used when listing the clusters of knowledge and skills. Since this practice is difficult to avoid and is characteristic of this type of listing, it should be of no concern. The writer of a competency curriculum must constantly keep in mind that a detailed listing of the competencies to be mastered by the novice is being developed. Each broad listing that you include in the curriculum development process focuses on competencies which the students must develop to be employable. Be thorough in your listings—it will pay off later.

The remainder of the description for the job title of rough carpenter from the *DOT* follows. Read it and relate to it the list of broad skill clusters which immediately follows the description. Compare the two to determine how the listing was compiled from the *DOT* description.

Cuts and assembles timbers to build trestles and cofferdams. Builds falsework to temporarily strengthen, protect, or disguise buildings undergoing construction. Erects scaffolding for buildings and ship structures and installs ladders, hand-rails, walkways, platforms, and gangways. Installs door and window bucks (rough frames in which finished frames are inserted) in designated positions in building framework, and braces them with boards nailed to framework. Installs subflooring in buildings. Nails plaster grounds (wood or metal strips) to stud-ding to provide guide for PLASTERER (const.). Fits and nails sheathing (first covering of boards) on outer walls and roofs of buildings.

19. The ability to cut and assemble timbers to build trestles.
20. The ability to construct ladders.
21. The ability to construct handrails.
22. The ability to construct walkways, platforms, and gangways.
23. The ability and knowledge to construct and properly insert window bucks.
24. The ability and knowledge to construct and properly insert door bucks.
25. The ability and knowledge to properly cut and install sub-flooring for buildings.
26. The ability and knowledge to properly cut and install sheathing for walls and roofs.
27. The ability and knowledge to nail plaster grounds (wood or metal strips) to studding to provide a guide for the plasterer.

You should note that the instructor in our example has chosen not to list certain skills, such as "erecting scaffolding for ships." The in-structor would not need to include this, or any other skill, if it is not required under a particular job title in the local employment commu-nity.

You may now draw on other resources to assist you in the task of listing and reviewing the broad sets of proficiencies for a job title.

2. *Refer to state curriculum guides.* Course guides from state de-partments of education can also be useful tools when listing clusters of knowledge and skills for a competency-based instruction system. The information contained in them, however, may not be as detailed as the curriculum writer desires. These manuals or guides tend to focus more on topical course content, rather than specific perform-ance tasks or job titles. They can be of help, however, in filling in some of the gaps that may exist in a list of broad skills and knowledge that has already been compiled from other sources.

These guides have been developed to include a course description that covers many job titles. Consequently, the instructor, as a curriculum writer, is faced with extracting useful material from a profusion of information included in the guide.

A course outline taken from a state curriculum guide for carpentry is provided here for your examination:

PROGRAM TITLE: CARPENTRY
COURSE NUMBER: 27418
COURSE OBJECTIVE: This specialized program is designed to enable persons to acquire the skills and knowledge necessary for initial employment in carpentry.

PROGRAM DESCRIPTION: Instruction includes experiences in the different phases of construction carpentry. Included in this program is training in fabrication, assembly, installation, and repair of structural units; common systems of frame construction and principles involved; blueprint reading; drafting; *applied mathematics; materials estimating;* and interpretation of building codes. Emphasis is placed on the use of carpentry tools, equipment, and materials.

Some sets of skills and knowledge which were not previously included in our list for rough carpenter may be inferred from this course description. Much of this description, though, is intended to be very general and is not designed for specific and specialized job titles. The following additions were identified by the instructor using the state curriculum guide:

28. The ability to use necessary construction mathematics.
29. The ability to accurately estimate the amount and cost of materials for a particular job.

The curriculum writer has excluded information about drafting and building codes contained in the state curriculum guide as they are not appropriate to the job title of rough carpenter.

3. *Examine textbooks.* The instructor in our "Developmental Example" would also want to examine textbooks for information applicable to the job title of rough carpenter. Texts are often general in scope and do not always focus on a specific occupation or job title. They are, however, a helpful resource for listing the theory knowledge which must be mastered by students wishing to become occupationally proficient.

Some examples follow of what might be gained from referring to published texts in carpentry when seeking additional sets of skills and knowledge for the job title of rough carpenter:

30. The knowledge and ability to identify various types of wood.
31. Knowledge concerning the various properties of different types of wood.
32. The ability and skill to determine a plot layout.

Though textbooks can be helpful, the curriculum writer has to be careful that the knowledge taken from books really pertains to the specific requirements of the occupation or job title for which the curriculum is being written.

POWER TOOL INSTITUTE, INC.

Illustration 14. In order to be occupationally proficient, the carpentry trainee must master a broad range of skills including the safe and proper use of power tools.

4. *Use manufacturers' handbooks and technical manuals.* Manufacturers' handbooks and technical manuals are probably the least used source for curriculum development. They can be extremely helpful, however, because they are specially prepared for persons employed in the field. They tend to include related information on the use and maintenance of equipment and materials.

Examples of additional input which can be gained from technical manuals and manufacturers' handbooks for the job title of rough carpenter are:

33. The ability to maintain radial arm saws properly.
34. The ability to maintain circular saws properly.
35. The ability and skill to troubleshoot and perform minor repairs on radial arm saws.
36. The ability and skill to troubleshoot and perform minor repairs on circular saws.

Technical information that relates to the maintenance, operation, and care of equipment is important. The entry-level employee must have some of this knowledge. The wise curriculum writer should make good use of a variety of these resources. Students should be introduced to the manuals and technical handbooks that are available so that they will be able to find any information they may later need on the job.

5. *Get help from trade associations and unions.* Various occupations have trade associations or unions affiliated with them. These groups are normally dedicated to improving the quality of the working lives of their members, as well as their members' knowledge of the job. Usually the members of these organizations are more than happy to assist an instructor.

There are two types of organizations which may be able to help the instructor in our "Developmental Example": carpenters' unions and contractors' associations. Examples of the kind of information that they may be able to provide for the instructor analyzing the job title of rough carpenter are:

37. The knowledge of how to function safely on the job site.
38. The knowledge and ability to cut costs by using building materials efficiently.
39. The ability and skill to maintain quality control standards on the job.

The knowledge that you can gain from individuals who are actually working in a field will tend to be practical and directly related to performance on the job. You should place a high value on any information that you obtain from these people.

6. *Draw on personal expertise.* You may be able to help your students more in the "tricks of the trade" department than in any other area. You can add a great deal of practicality to the program by drawing on your own experience when designing the curriculum.

Examples of the types of knowledge that a carpentry instructor with trade experience could add to the clusters already listed are:

40. The skill to nail fasteners of all types into different kinds of building materials for extended periods of time without fatigue.
41. The skill to fabricate and properly use templates.
42. The ability and knowledge necessary to obtain and maintain a well-stocked set of personal tools.

7. *Consult your advisory committee.* There is probably only one other source of information which is as valuable as your own experience and the experience of persons employed in the field. That resource is the experience and advice to be gained from an active and interested program advisory committee. Advisory committee involvement in curriculum development should be sought at all levels. The advisory committee can be used as a primary source for listing broad skills and knowledge and can perform a validating role for the curriculum as well. There is a sound reason for this.

Ideally, members of your advisory committee represent employers in your local area since these individuals are the people your students must please in order to obtain entry-level employment. The instructor should never lose sight of the fact that the purpose of any occupational instruction program is to prepare students for employment. Advisory committee members should have an opportunity to examine the proposed curriculum at all stages in the development of the competency-based instruction system. The first opportunity for such an examination is at the stage when tentative sets of knowledge and skills for the occupation have been specified.

Each advisory committee member should be presented with a list of occupational proficiencies which have been gathered from all of the other sources. A survey form similar to the one shown in Illustration 15 could be used.

Listed below are groups of skills and knowledge. Please review each entry and indicate how important it is for an individual to develop each skill to become employable as a *rough carpenter* in our community.

DESCRIPTION OF SKILL OR KNOWLEDGE	NOT IMPORTANT	SHOULD KNOW	VERY IMPORTANT
1. Constructing forms	☐	☐	☐
2. Constructing scaffolds	☐	☐	☐
3. Constructing tunnel and sewer supports	☐	☐	☐
4. Constructing temporary frame shelters	☐	☐	☐
5. Using construction power tools	☐	☐	☐
6. Interpreting blueprints	☐	☐	☐
7. Making precision measurements and cuts	☐	☐	☐
8. Using a steel tape measure	☐	☐	☐
9. Using a framing square	☐	☐	☐
10. Determining dimensions	☐	☐	☐

DESCRIPTION OF SKILL OR KNOWLEDGE	NOT IMPORTANT	SHOULD KNOW	VERY IMPORTANT
11. Securely fastening structures	☐	☐	☐
12. Selecting proper fasteners	☐	☐	☐
13. Bracing concrete forms with lumber	☐	☐	☐
14. Bracing forms with tie rods and bolts	☐	☐	☐
15. Forming concrete piers	☐	☐	☐
16. Forming concrete footings	☐	☐	☐
17. Forming concrete walls	☐	☐	☐
18. Constructing pouring chutes	☐	☐	☐
19. Cutting and assembling trestles	☐	☐	☐
20. Constructing ladders	☐	☐	☐
21. Constructing handrails	☐	☐	☐

	NOT IMPORTANT	SHOULD KNOW	VERY IMPORTANT
DESCRIPTION OF SKILL OR KNOWLEDGE			
32. Laying out a plot	☐	☐	☐
33. Maintaining a radial arm saw	☐	☐	☐
34. Maintaining a circular saw	☐	☐	☐
35. Troubleshooting radial arm saws	☐	☐	☐
36. Troubleshooting circular saws	☐	☐	☐
37. Functioning safely on the job	☐	☐	☐
38. Efficiently using building materials	☐	☐	☐
39. Maintaining quality control	☐	☐	☐
40. Nailing without fatigue	☐	☐	☐
41. Making and using templates	☐	☐	☐
42. Maintaining a set of tools	☐	☐	☐

	NOT IMPORTANT	SHOULD KNOW	VERY IMPORTANT
DESCRIPTION OF SKILL OR KNOWLEDGE			
22. Constructing walkways, platforms, and gangways	☐	☐	☐
23. Constructing and inserting window bucks	☐	☐	☐
24. Constructing and inserting door bucks	☐	☐	☐
25. Cutting and installing subflooring	☐	☐	☐
26. Cutting and installing sheathing	☐	☐	☐
27. Nailing plaster grounds to studding	☐	☐	☐
28. Using construction mathematics	☐	☐	☐
29. Estimating material costs	☐	☐	☐
30. Identifying types of wood	☐	☐	☐
31. Knowledge of wood properties	☐	☐	☐

Please list any additional sets of skills and knowledge which might be required of a *rough carpenter* in our community that are not listed above.

Illustration 15. Curriculum Validation

Ask advisory committee members whether each set of knowledge and skills which you have listed is actually required by them of entry-level employees. They will be glad to tell you. They may also make some suggestions for adding more entries to your list. There is no better way to lay the groundwork for validation of a curriculum than to involve advisory committee members in the developmental stages.

Examples of the types of knowledge that advisory committee members might be able to provide are:

43. The ability and knowledge to set up a work area properly.
44. The ability and knowledge to clean up a work site properly.
45. The ability and knowledge to spot and report potential problems to a supervisor.
46. The ability to display the proper work attitude.

Most of the information which is obtained from employers on your advisory committee is practical and important in the real world of profit and loss. It would not be unusual for one of your advisory committee members to completely surprise you with a suggestion that you would not have anticipated, such as: "The ability to install aluminum gutters on residences."

The clusters of skills and knowledge that advisory committee members indicate as not important should be dropped or reevaluated. Proficiencies which they indicate as important, but which have not been listed in the survey, should be added.

REVIEW QUESTIONS

1. What is meant by the phrase "broad set of knowledge and skills"?

2. Name the possible resources which can be used to develop a list of skills and knowledge for a job title.

3. Discuss how the information contained in the *DOT* for a particular job title can be used to begin to develop a list of broad skills and knowledge.

4. Must the instructor use all of the information contained in the *DOT* for a particular job title?

5. Textbooks are particularly useful tools for the curriculum writer when identifying what type of knowledge?

6. Describe how advisory committee members can help in developing a list of broad sets of skills and knowledge.

CHAPTER

Writing
Competency
Statements

FOUR

THE first two steps in the development of a competency-based curriculum are the systematic selection of a job title and the listing of broad sets of knowledge and skills which are required in that occupation. The procedures to be followed in the first two phases have already been discussed in earlier chapters. The next step in the conversion of your curriculum to one which focuses on the performance of specific skills is the writing of competency statements for each set of knowledge and skills. This stage of the curriculum revision process is critical because the competency statement is the foundation on which you and your students base all learning activities. The writing of competency statements which carefully describe satisfactory standards of proficiency for employability is also important because it clearly defines the goal that the student and the instructor hope to achieve.

The following questions will be answered in this chapter:

What is a competency statement?

How do you write a competency statement?

What are the critical factors to consider when writing a list of job title competencies?

The answers to these questions will help you to write sound competency statements and to design appropriate learning activities.

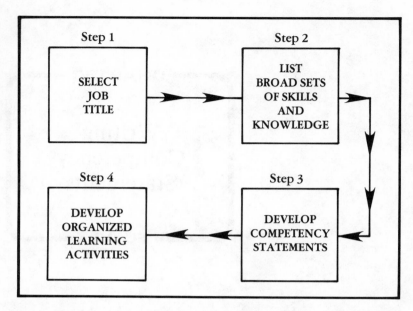

Illustration 16. Flow chart for the development of a competency-based instruction system.

What Is a Competency Statement?

The definition of *occupational competency* which we developed in the first chapter is: ''A specific job skill that an employer expects an employee to possess in order to obtain and maintain employment.'' Focusing on the precise meaning of this phrase should emphasize the importance of the proper approach when writing occupational competency statements.

A *competency statement* is a written phrase or sentence which communicates to the reader (student) the precise degree of skill or performance which is required for a particular occupational skill. A complete list of competency statements for a job title ideally represents a detailed listing of the skills and knowledge which are required for employment in that occupation.

Competency statements that are properly written for classroom or laboratory use in occupational instruction programs meet the following criteria:

They clearly describe the skill to be mastered.
They specify how skill attainment is to be demonstrated to
  the instructor.
They include a measurable standard.
They are concise.

DEVELOPMENTAL EXAMPLE: Part 3
Writing Competency Statements

Let's examine a competency statement which might be used in a job title curriculum for rough carpenter.

> The student will demonstrate proficiency using a steel tape to measure accurately the dimensions of a structure specified by the instructor. Standard: 100 percent accuracy.

Each of the above-mentioned criteria for a competency statement has been met in this sample. The accurate use of a steel tape measure is clearly specified as the skill that must be mastered. The competency statement clearly communicates to the student how this proficiency is to be demonstrated. A standard of 100 percent accuracy is specified and everything is stated in one sentence.

The criteria listed above should be met in each competency statement in an occupational instruction program. Writing competencies in this manner helps to enhance the many advantages associated with a competency-based instruction system. Let's examine how each of the four criteria can be met when writing competency statements.

Clearly describe the skill to be mastered. The preceding chapter described how to derive broad lists of knowledge and skills for a job title. An example of one cluster of skills and knowledge for the occupational classification of rough carpenter, which was selected in our "Developmental Example," originally appeared as follows:

> The ability to use various construction power tools.

The reader does not have to be familiar with the specific duties of a rough carpenter to perceive that more than one set of competencies related to the use of power tools must be mastered by the student who wishes to become proficient with the equipment that is used by a rough carpenter in the construction trade. In fact, the student would need to become skilled in using a variety of power tools.

Assume that the carpentry instructor in the preceding example determined that a rough carpenter in the local community needed to become proficient only with the following power tools:

> The circular saw
> The electric drill
> The saber saw
> The electric plane
> The radial arm saw

The instructor's responsibility at this point is to indicate to the students, in the form of competency statements, that they must be proficient with each piece of equipment to be employable in this occupation. Eventually, there will be a series of competencies written for each of the various power tools that must be mastered.

Specify how skill attainment is to be demonstrated. The students in our "Developmental Example" obviously must demonstrate that they know how to operate each of the five types of power tools which were mentioned. The conditions under and methods by which they will demonstrate this skill attainment determine the pattern, wording, and structure of the competency statements which are to be written.

The following statements, for example, describe the numerous conditions under which the student will prove competency in operating the circular saw:

1. Demonstrate the safe use of the circular saw.
2. Demonstrate skill in making bevel adjustments on the circular saw for joinings as specified by the instructor.
3. Demonstrate skill in making a freehand cut along a predetermined line using the circular saw.
4. Demonstrate skill in making 10 precision rip cuts on the various types of lumber which are most often used by rough carpenters.
5. Demonstrate skill in making 10 precision crosscuts on the various types of lumber which are most often used by rough carpenters.
6. Demonstrate the competent use of the circular saw in making precision cuts on advanced construction projects as specified by the instructor.

The reader should recognize at this point that one simple cluster of knowledge and skills (in this case the ability to use construction power tools) can be expanded into a number of competencies merely by defining the conditions under which the student will demonstrate this occupational proficiency. There could be an almost unlimited number of conditions under or tests through which the student will demonstrate the attainment of the employability standard for a broad cluster of skills and knowledge.

All of the possible conditions under which your students might be asked to demonstrate mastery of broad skill clusters should be considered and must ultimately be included in the list of competency statements you are developing. You can see, as was mentioned in an earlier chapter, that one of the heaviest costs in developing a competency-based instruction system is the amount of time and effort that an instructor must expend in planning the program.

Include a measurable standard. The third element that a competency statement must contain is a prestated and measurable standard. That measure must be an *actual quantity that can be tabulated.* The measurable standard can be either an objective standard (such as a measurement taken from a pressure gauge, ruler, or micrometer), or some type of rating system (such as a five-point rating scale).

The main reason that a competency statement should contain a measurable standard is for the purpose of evaluation. The measurable standard is the only way that the instructor and the student know whether the desired level of proficiency as specified in the competency statement has been met.

Students who enroll in a carpentry program and plan to become rough carpenters should be expected to meet several sets of standards relating to the use of power tools. Standards must be assigned for each of the conditions under which students will demonstrate proficiency. The measurable standards which could be included for each of the tasks or conditions related to the use of the circular saw are illustrated in the following examples:

1. *When demonstrating the safe use of the circular saw,* the student must achieve a minimum performance rating of "5" (on a scale of 1-5).
2. *In making bevel adjustments,* the joinings of the lumber, for which the cuts were made, must produce an opening of less than 1/16th of an inch.
3. *When demonstrating skill in freehand guiding of the circular saw,* the student must achieve a minimum performance rating of "5" (on a scale of 1-5).

4. *In making 10 precision rip cuts on the various types of lumber which are typically used by rough carpenters,* the cut made by the student is within 1/32nd of an inch of the dimensions specified by the instructor.

5. *In making 10 precision crosscuts on the various types of lumber which are typically used by rough carpenters,* the cut made by the student is within 1/32nd of an inch of the specified dimensions.

6. *When using the circular saw to make precision cuts required on advanced construction projects as specified by the instructor,* the student must achieve a minimum performance rating of "4" (on a scale of 1-5).

The two types of measurable standards used in the preceding examples are a rating scale of five points and the type of measurable standard which states "to within 1/32nd of an inch" or "to within 1/16th of an inch." The measurement or standard associated with a competency must be quantifiable. This feature makes it possible to assess the degree of student achievement.

Make them concise. The purpose in writing a competency statement is to communicate to students the specific skill level that they need to possess to be employable. The conditions under which students must demonstrate proficiency are expressed and a standard against which their performance is measured is included in the written competency statement. There is little reason for any other information to be contained in the competency statement.

An economy of words should be practiced faithfully by the writer of competency statements. The fewer the words, the clearer the message. Compare the following example of a poorly written competency statement with the one that is written concisely. Both contain everything that has been cited as necessary for producing effective competency statements, but there is a sharp difference in readability between them. Which of the following competency statements do *you* feel could be better understood?

> The student will gather a number of 2 × 4s after asking the instructor from what storage pile to take them and read the plans and make accurate cuts to within 1/32nd of an inch and be certain that the instructor measures all boards; then build a 10-foot section of stud wall using the plans that the instructor gives to the student.

or,

The student will build a 10-foot stud wall out of 2 x 4s cut to within 1/32nd of an inch accuracy using specifications supplied by the instructor.

You can easily see that the second example is far superior to the first example, which is so poorly organized that confusion will surely result. A student who is presented with a list of brief and specific competency statements will recognize easily what is going to be required and should respond more positively to the learning activity. An instructor of occupational skills must capitalize as much as possible on this kind of motivational advantage—an advantage which is central to the system of competency-based instruction.

Illustration 17. In this vocational program students are able to develop and refine carpentry skills by actually building a house in the "classroom."

How Do You Write a Competency Statement?

A four-step method should be followed when writing competency statements:

1. Analyze each broad set of proficiencies that is associated with a job title and identify clearly the skills to be mastered.
2. Specify the conditions under which the student will demonstrate skill attainment.
3. Assign measurable, entry-level standards for each of the skills to be mastered.
4. Combine all of the essentials into a single sentence.

Let's examine each of the steps more closely.

1. *Analyze each broad set of proficiencies that is associated with a job title and identify clearly the skills to be mastered.* The instructor who is involved in the writing of competency statements should think of them as if they were test items or questions. Examine each of the broad sets of skills and knowledge that are required for employability under the job title you have selected, and identify the specific skills a student must possess to demonstrate competency.

The following is an example of one of the broad sets of knowledge which was identified by an instructor in an electrical wiring program as necessary for a student to be qualified to seek employment as an electrician:

> The student must possess the ability to connect service wires to a building service entrance.

The service wires, supplied by the utility company, bring electrical power from the main lines to a building. At a specific location, which is commonly referred to as the service entrance, the service wires are connected to the building's electrical circuits. The student must become competent, as the broad set of knowledge states, in connecting service wires to the service entrance of the building.

The instructor of the electrical wiring class must now isolate specific integral tasks that the students must be able to perform to be considered thoroughly competent in connecting service wires to the service entrance. These tasks then become the basis for listing conditions under which competence in the broad skill cluster will be demonstrated to the instructor.

2. *Specify the conditions under which the student will demonstrate skill attainment.* The listing of the conditions under which students will demonstrate occupational proficiency can be quite difficult. The instructor must consider not only the tasks to be performed but also the circumstances or conditions under which students will show their level of skill attainment. The conditions under which students will be demonstrating their proficiency must be similar to those faced on the job in order to ultimately be a valid and comprehensive measure. The provisions for skills testing must be complete and appropriate for the desired competency, and must be administrable within the limits of the available resources.

Reread the example given above in Step 1 of a broad set of knowledge for the electrical wiring class. This statement specifies that students in the class must demonstrate to the instructor that they can connect the utility company's wires to the service entrance of a building. Since this is a critical procedure, requiring an integrated set of specialized skills and knowledge, it is understandable that clarity and precision are necessary when outlining conditions for competency testing.

The instructor might select the following tasks in which student competence will be demonstrated:

> Connecting the service entrance
> Installing the electric meter
> Attaching conduit to a service entrance
> Wiring a circuit breaker panel
> Grounding the installation

In each of the five tasks mentioned above the student-electrician uses job-related skills to demonstrate competency in connecting the service entrance wires to a building service entrance.

The conditions under which occupational competence must be verified should be listed for each broad set of skills and knowledge in the job title curriculum. These conditions can actually be considered as performance tests. This is a critical step in the development of performance-based, measurable competency statements.

3. *Assign measurable, entry-level standards for each of the skills to be mastered.* A competency statement should be written in such a way that the student knows what is acceptable performance and the instructor has no difficulty in measuring skill achievement. The instructor must be able to tabulate the results of skill testing based on

the assigned standard.

Some possible measures or standards for the skills outlined in the electrical wiring program are italicized in the tentative competency statements listed below:

1. Perform all critical connections between the service wires and the service entrance wires of a building *with 100 percent conformance to electrical code specifications.*
2. Install the electric meter to a building service entrance *according to manufacturer's specifications.*
3. Achieve *a minimum performance rating of "3"* (on a scale of 1-5) when demonstrating proficiency in the cutting and reaming of conduit so that it is free of burrs.
4. Achieve *a minimum performance rating of "3"* (on a scale of 1-5) when demonstrating skill in attaching electrical conduit at building service entrance.
5. Perform all critical connections when wiring a circuit breaker panel *with 100 percent conformance to electrical code specifications.*
6. Achieve *a minimum performance rating of "5"* (on a scale of 1-5) when demonstrating proficiency in the proper grounding of service entrance installations.

4. *Combine all of the essentials into a single sentence.* Broad sets of knowledge were identified and analyzed for the electrical wiring program. Conditions for the competency tests were outlined and measurable standards were assigned to each test. The combination of all of the essential elements into a concise and cohesive sentence is all that remains to be done in the process of writing a competency statement.

We will now examine a competency statement which might be used to determine if a student in an electrical wiring class can competently perform the task of connecting service wires to a building service entrance.

1. The student will make all critical connections between the service wires and the service entrance wires of a building with 100 percent conformance to electrical code specifications.

This task description includes all of the elements of a sound competency statement. The skill to be performed is *to make connections between wires.* The conditions (or performance test) are that *the connections will be made between the service entrance wires of a building and the power company's service wires.* The standard or unit of measure is *100 percent conformance to electrical code specifications.*

The competency statements which remain for our electrical wiring program example are listed below. Read them and attempt to identify the three elements of a competency statement which are to be included:

2. The student will demonstrate proficiency in the installation of an electric meter to a building service entrance according to manufacturer's specifications.
3. The student will achieve a minimum performance rating of "3" (on a scale of 1-5) when demonstrating proficiency in the cutting and reaming of conduit so that it is free of burrs.
4. The student will achieve a minimum performance rating of "3" (on a scale of 1-5) when demonstrating skill in attaching electrical conduit at the building service entrance.
5. The student will demonstrate proficiency in performing all critical connections when wiring a circuit breaker panel with 100 percent conformance to electrical code specifications.
6. The student will achieve a minimum performance rating of "5" (on a scale of 1-5) when demonstrating proficiency in the proper grounding of service entrance installations.

What Are the Critical Factors to Consider When Writing a List of Job Title Competencies?

An instructor who is converting to a competency-based curriculum must always keep in mind that a competency statement describes a test for competency. Competency statements can be properly thought of as the "test questions" of occupational instruction. The instructor should make use of sound educational measurement methods and techniques in order to insure the accountability of the program and the employability of the students. Two critical factors to consider when formulating competency statements are that they:

Use sound techniques of measurement
Are reliable and measure exactly what they are designed to measure

A discussion of each of these important factors follows.

Use sound techniques of measurement. Competency statements which contain measurable standards can generally be classified into two broad categories: objectively measured competencies and subjectively measured competencies. We will examine each category.

Objectively measured competencies. This type of competency statement includes a standard that can be measured so that it leaves little room for interpretation or error. This written performance standard can be measured with a device such as a ruler or a thermometer, or may be scored through a written test.

An assessment of competency made with an instrument can be referred to as a "direct objective measure" of student skill performance. An example is:

> The student will demonstrate proficiency in reading the blood pressure of a patient with 100 percent accuracy.

In this example the student will demonstrate a manipulative skill which can then be checked with an instrument and verified by the instructor with a great degree of accuracy. All competencies which are classified as objectively measured involve the same type of relationship, that is, the measurement of a prestated standard with some type of instrument or scoring method.

Other examples of direct objective measuring devices are the carpenter's level, a ruler, a tape measure, and a protractor. A chef may use a measuring cup and spoon and an electrician has meters which measure the proper functioning of connections and circuits. The same kinds of direct objective measures may be made of competencies for most occupations.

A written examination that can be scored by a measurable and equitable method is also an objective measure of competency. The results are generally expressed in terms of minimum scores. Here is an example of a competency statement that includes a written test which is a direct objective measure:

> The student will score a minimum of 90 percent on an objective examination related to the theory of an internal combustion engine.

Speed is another kind of objectively measured standard that can be used to rate student performance. Speed, as measured in minutes and seconds, can be used as an objective measure of a competency. Instructors in office education programs, for example, use time as a criterion of student performance for some skills, as in this example:

The student must type for a period of 5 minutes at a minimum of 50 words per minute with 5 or fewer errors.

Other occupational fields also use time standards. Students may not be considered employable in some occupations unless they can perform certain tasks within a reasonable time. It is possible, for example, that a machine operator will be required to produce a specified number of units per hour to meet minimum employability standards.

Illustration 18. This student uses a self-instructional audiovisual package to help improve speed and accuracy.

Subjectively measured competencies. Many skills that an entry-level employee must possess cannot be directly measured with a device or by a series of questions on a written examination. The student who is studying marketing and sales, for example, must possess the skill necessary to project a certain pleasantness to potential customers. Salespeople must also be ready to help customers make up their minds but must not appear pushy. They must exude a certain demeanor, develop a sense of timing in relation to making the sale, and be able to offer advice on a product without seeming overeager.

The instructor in a marketing program must spend a great deal of time helping students to develop these skills which are difficult to measure objectively. The skills necessary to make a sale relate to attitude, personality, and the development of a sixth sense for anticipating consumer behavior.

Employers in all occupational fields look for certain intangible skills and attitudes in entry-level employes. The instructor who is converting to a competency-based curriculum must not ignore the importance of specifying these special skills in the form of competency statements and must allow for measuring fairly and equitably the degree to which the students acquire these special skills.

One method of evaluating subjective skills and attitudes is to use a scoring device known as a rating scale. The instructor should identify the subjective skills to be acquired by students. A rating system, which attaches a measurable standard to subjective skill attainment, should be developed so that an evaluation of the students' performance can take place. Some rating systems use words and phrases and others use numbers. Examples of each of these two types are shown in Illustration 19.

```
                      RATING SCALES

      Example 1                          Example 2
      (Words)                            (Numbers)

      _____ Excellent                  _____ 5

      _____ Good                       _____ 4

      _____ Fair                       _____ 3

      _____ Poor                       _____ 2

                                         _____ 1
```

Illustration 19. Examples of Rating Scales

An example of a subjectively measured competency using a rating scale to establish proficiency standards follows:

> The student will achieve *a minimum performance rating of "good"* when demonstrating proficiency in building and closing a sale.

The instructor should exercise caution when using rating scales. Every effort should be made to eliminate teacher bias. The instructor must strive to assess those skills, which can be observed but cannot be objectively measured with an instrument or test, accurately and equitably.

The general areas of proficiency for which the writer of competency statements will rate student performance subjectively are quality of performance, technique, and attitude.

The *quality of performance* is the level of proficiency which the employer requires an entry-level employee to have in order to obtain and maintain employment. The notion of a "minimum acceptable performance" is one standard which the occupational educator should always keep in mind when writing competency statements. We will examine subjective rating scales in greater detail in a later chapter.

The *technique* that the student demonstrates when performing a specified task is another important factor to be considered in competency evaluation. Improper technique can affect safety, efficiency, and, ultimately, the employability of a student. The instructor should demonstrate for the student the technique that is considered acceptable and should hold students accountable for mastering the technique as demonstrated. The following example is a competency statement for an electronics class in which technique is evaluated:

> The student will achieve a minimum performance rating of "4" (on a scale of 1-5) when demonstrating the proper technique for soldering an electrical connection.

Attitude is also an important subjectively measured competency which should be considered in an evaluation of skill attainment. Many employers consider a proper work attitude to be as important as the possession of technical skills. A highly skilled employee with a poor work attitude is, after all, a less than desirable employee. The instructor should include every conceivable measure of attitude when writing occupational competency statements for a job title curriculum.

Are reliable and measure exactly what they are designed to measure. Competency statements must be valid. They must measure precisely what they are intended to measure. The importance of clearly stated goals as a motivating factor in competency-based programs reinforces this need for precision when writing competency statements.

Here is an example of a competency statement which would have low validity:

> The student will demonstrate a knowledge of stacking lumber by size in less than 30 minutes.

What is the instructor attempting to measure? Is it the student's strength or the student's knowledge or skill attainment?

The competency statement given above was intended to measure the student's knowledge of the various sizes of lumber, but does not clearly express this. It states that the student has 30 minutes in which to stack lumber. The instructor, however, would not normally be interested only in how quickly the student could sort and stack lumber. The competency statement is therefore not properly designed to measure what it is intended to measure.

The writer of a competency statement must thoroughly analyze the nature of the skill that is to be mastered. The more accurately the competency test reflects the character and quality of skill performance, the more valid the competency statement will be as a basis for the evaluation of student proficiency and the effectiveness of the program. We will now return to our "Developmental Example" and examine how these principles are applied in this program.

DEVELOPMENTAL EXAMPLE: Part 4
Identifying Specific Skills and
Assigning Performance Standards

Earlier in this chapter one of the examples of the broad clusters of skills and knowledge that a rough carpenter must develop was examined. In this example students were expected to master the competencies associated with the development of the following broad set of skills and knowledge.

> The ability to use construction power tools.

Our analysis of this cluster disclosed that there are five types of construction power tools which the rough carpenter must learn to use in order to be employable. Those tools are:

The circular saw	The electric plane
The electric drill	The radial arm saw
The saber saw	

The next step in the development of written competency statements for the use of these tools is to list the integral tasks involved in their use and conditions under which competence is to be shown.

The conditions under which the student will demonstrate proficiency in the use of a circular saw are restated from earlier in this chapter followed by those for the other tools:

1. Demonstrate the safe use of the circular saw.
2. Demonstrate skill in making bevel adjustments on the circular saw for joinings as specified by the instructor.
3. Demonstrate skill in making a freehand cut along a predetermined line using the circular saw.
4. Demonstrate skill in making 10 precision rip cuts on the various types of lumber which are most often used by rough carpenters.
5. Demonstrate skill in making 10 precision crosscuts on the various types of lumber which are most often used by rough carpenters.
6. Demonstrate the competent use of the circular saw in making precision cuts on advanced construction projects as specified by the instructor.

The *electric drill:*

7. Demonstrate the safe use of the electric drill.
8. Demonstrate the skill necessary to properly change drill bits.
9. Demonstrate the proper technique to be used when boring 10 different holes as specified by the instructor.
10. Demonstrate proper maintenance and care of the electric drill.

The *saber saw:*

11. Demonstrate the safe use of the saber saw.
12. Demonstrate the skill necessary to select and properly change cutting blades.
13. Demonstrate skill in cutting curves on wood as specified by the instructor.
14. Demonstrate skill in using a saber saw to do bevel cutting.
15. Demonstrate the use of the saber saw in cutting metal.

The *electric plane:*

16. Demonstrate the safe use of the electric plane.
17. Demonstrate the use of the electric plane to plane window casings.

18. Demonstrate the use of the electric plane to plane door casings.
19. Demonstrate the use of the electric plane in five construction-related problems as specified by the instructor.

The *radial arm saw:*

20. Demonstrate the safe use of the radial arm saw.
21. Demonstrate the use of the radial arm saw to make 10 precision crosscuts to dimensions supplied by the instructor.
22. Demonstrate proficiency in adjusting the mechanism to make angular cuts.
23. Demonstrate proficiency in adjusting the mechanism to make miter cuts.
24. Demonstrate proficiency in adjusting the depth of cuts.
25. Demonstrate proficiency in using the radial arm saw to perform rip cuts.
26. Demonstrate proficiency in using the radial arm saw to do bevel cuts.

The instructor in the "Developmental Example" has listed a total of 26 separate conditions under which skill proficiency is to be tested. The next step in the process of writing competencies is to assign a performance standard to each of the testing conditions that have been mentioned above. This can be done by using the scoring methods and techniques for objective and subjective evaluation that were discussed earlier in this chapter.

After a measurable standard has been assigned for each competency, the only task which remains is to write the competency statement. Following are some of the competency statements for the broad set of skills and knowledge identified under the job title of rough carpenter. These task assignments must be fulfilled for the student to be considered proficient in the use of the power tools. The complete competency statements for the use of power tools are listed below.

The *circular saw:*

1. The student will achieve a minimum performance rating of "5" (on a scale of 1-5) when demonstrating the safe use of the circular saw.
2. The student will demonstrate skill in using the circular saw to make bevel cuts which will join with an opening of less than 1/16th of an inch.

3. The student will achieve a minimum performance rating of "5" (on a scale of 1-5) when demonstrating proficiency in making a freehand cut along a predetermined line with the circular saw.
4. The student will make 10 rip cuts with the circular saw on various types of lumber to within 1/32nd of an inch of the dimensions specified by the instructor.
5. The student will make 10 crosscuts with the circular saw on various types of lumber to within 1/32nd of an inch of the dimensions specified by the instructor.
6. The student will achieve a minimum performance rating of "4" (on a scale of 1-5) when demonstrating the use of the circular saw on five advanced construction projects as specified by the instructor.

POWER TOOL INSTITUTE, INC.

Illustration 20. Safety is important when learning to use tools and should always be included when writing competency statements for those tools.

The *electric drill:*

7. The student will achieve a minimum performance rating of "5" when demonstrating proficiency in the safe use of the electric drill.
8. The student will achieve a minimum performance rating of "5" when demonstrating proficiency in changing electric drill bits.
9. The student will achieve a minimum performance rating of "4" when demonstrating the proper technique in using the electric drill to bore 10 holes as specified by the instructor.
10. The student will achieve a minimum performance rating of "4" when demonstrating the proper maintenance and care of the electric drill.

The *saber saw:*

11. The student will achieve a minimum performance rating of "5" when demonstrating proficiency in the safe use of the saber saw.
12. The student will achieve a minimum performance rating of "5" when demonstrating skill in selecting and changing saber saw blades.
13. The student will achieve a minimum performance rating of "4" when demonstrating skill in cutting curves on wood as specified by the instructor.
14. The student will demonstrate skill in using the saber saw to make bevel cuts so that the joining has an opening of 1/16th of an inch or less.
15. The student will demonstrate skill in cutting metal with the saber saw to within 1/32nd of an inch of the dimensions supplied by the instructor.

The *electric plane:*

16. The student will achieve a minimum performance rating of "5" when demonstrating the safe use of the electric plane.
17. The student will demonstrate skill in using the electric plane to plane window casings to within 1/16th of an inch of the specified dimensions.
18. The student will demonstrate skill in using the electric plane to plane door casings to within 1/16th of an inch of the specified dimension.
19. The student will achieve a minimum performance rating of "4" when using the electric plane on five advanced con-

struction projects specified by the instructor.

The *radial arm saw:*

20. The student will achieve a minimum performance rating of "5" when demonstrating the safe use of the radial arm saw.
21. The student will make 10 precision crosscuts to within 1/32nd of an inch of the dimensions specified by the instructor.
22. The student will demonstrate skill in adjusting the yoke of the radial arm saw to make angular cuts to within 1/16th of an inch of the dimensions supplied by the instructor.
23. The student will achieve a minimum performance rating of "4" when demonstrating proficiency in making miter cuts.
24. The student will achieve a minimum performance rating of "4" when demonstrating proficiency in adjusting the depth of cuts on the radial arm saw.
25. The student will demonstrate proficiency in making 10 rip-cuts to within 1/32nd of an inch of the dimensions supplied by the instructor.
26. The student will demonstrate proficiency in making bevel cuts so that the joining has an opening of 1/16th of an inch or less.

The process of writing competency statements is a difficult and time-consuming task. The instructor must be very careful that the conditions under which the students are to prove competence are appropriate. The competency statement itself must be clear and concise. Competencies must also be thorough and measure only the behavioral changes or skill performance which is required for obtaining and maintaining employment.

REVIEW QUESTIONS

1. Why is the actual process of writing competency statements so important?

2. What is a competency statement?

3. List and briefly explain the four criteria which a properly written competency contains.

4. Why is it important for each competency statement to specify how skill attainment is to be demonstrated?

5. Why should you list and record the specific tasks which have to be mastered for each broad cluster of knowledge and skills?

6. Why is it important for each competency statement to contain a measurable standard?

7. What is meant by the term "objectively measured competency"?

8. What is meant by the term "subjectively measured competency"?

CHAPTER

Developing and Sequencing Competency-Based Instruction Units

FIVE

TO review, the first step in converting to a competency-based curriculum is to identify a job title under which to prepare students. The second step is to list the broad sets of knowledge and skills which students must acquire to become employable. The third step is to write a list of performance objectives, in the form of competency statements, which are based on a detailed task analysis of the broad clusters of skills and knowledge.

Once the competency statements have been designed and written, following the guidelines discussed in the earlier chapters, the next major task is the development, structuring, and sequencing of instructional units which will help students achieve prestated occupational competencies. To do so the instructor must learn:

How do you identify appropriate instructional units for each competency?

How do you set up a course outline?

How do you develop organized learning activities?

How Do You Identify Appropriate Instructional Units for Each Competency?

The bulk of the work involved in identifying instructional units for a competency-based instruction system should already be complete, if the instructor has followed the steps of conversion which were recommended in the preceding chapters. The listing of broad sets of knowledge and skills can form the basis for the identification of the units of instruction which will eventually become a part of the course outline.

Condensed versions of the original broad skill and knowledge statements are sufficient to use when identifying and listing the units of instruction. Consider the following skill statement from the electrical wiring program used as an example in the previous chapter:

> The student must possess the ability to connect service wires to a building service entrance.

This statement can be condensed to provide the following title for an instructional unit: "Building Service Entrances." This title is merely a description derived from the central concept of the general occupational cluster statement.

The listing of the instructional units for the job title of rough carpenter are shown in the right-hand column in the following example. Read the statements of the broad clusters of occupational skills, which were developed in Chapter 3, in the left-hand column. Then compare the unit titles with the skill statements. Observe how these original statements are reduced to create brief titles for instructional units. These instructional unit titles are the basis for the course outline.

DEVELOPMENTAL EXAMPLE: Part 5
Titles of Instructional Units

The ability to construct basic forms for the pouring of concrete	Form Construction
The ability to construct scaffolds	Scaffold Construction
The ability to construct tunnel and sewer supports	Constructing Tunnel and Sewer Supports
The ability to construct temporary frame shelters	Constructing Temporary Frame Shelters
The ability to use portable power tools	Portable Power Tools
The ability to interpret blueprints	Blueprint Reading
The ability to make precision measurements and cuts	Measuring and Cutting

The ability to use a steel tape measure	The Steel Tape Measure
The ability to use a framing square	The Framing Square
The ability and knowledge to determine accurately the dimensions of a structure	Measuring a Structure
The ability to fasten wooden structures together properly	Fastening
The knowledge to select proper fasteners for various jobs	Selecting Fasteners
The ability and skill to properly brace concrete forms using lumber	Bracing with Lumber
The ability and skill to brace forms using tie rods and anchor bolts	Bracing with Tie Rods and Anchor Bolts
The knowledge and skill to form concrete piers of varying dimensions	Forming Concrete Piers
The knowledge and skill to form footings of varying dimensions	Forming Footings
The knowledge and skill to form walls of varying dimensions	Forming Walls
The ability to construct chutes properly for the pouring of concrete	Forming Pouring Chutes
The ability to cut and assemble timbers to build trestles	Constructing Trestles
The ability to construct ladders	Constructing Ladders
The ability to construct handrails	Constructing Handrails
The ability to construct walkways, platforms, and gangways	Constructing Walkways, Platforms, and Gangways
The ability and knowledge to construct and properly insert window bucks	Building and Inserting Window Bucks
The ability and knowledge to construct and properly insert door bucks	Building and Inserting Door Bucks
The ability and knowledge to properly cut and install subflooring	Cutting and Installing Subflooring
The ability and knowledge to properly cut and install sheathing for walls and roofs	Sheathing
The ability and knowledge to nail plaster grounds (wood or metal strips) to studding to provide a guide for the plasterer	Preparing Walls for Plastering

The ability to use necessary construction mathematics	Construction Mathematics
The ability to accurately estimate the amount and cost of materials needed for a particular job	Estimating the Amount and Cost of Materials
The knowledge and ability to identify various types of wood	Wood Identification
Knowledge concerning the various properties of different types of wood	Wood Properties
The ability and skill to determine plot layout	Plot Layout
The ability to maintain radial arm saws properly	Maintaining Radial Arm Saws
The ability to maintain circular saws properly	Maintaining Circular Saws
The ability and skill to troubleshoot and perform minor repairs on radial arm saws	Troubleshooting Radial Arm Saws
The ability and skill to troubleshoot and perform minor repairs on circular saws	Troubleshooting Circular Saws
The knowledge of how to function safely on the job site	Safety on the Job
The knowledge and ability to cut costs by using building materials efficiently	Cost Control
The ability and skill to maintain quality control standards on the job	Quality Control
The skill to nail fasteners of all types into different kinds of building materials for extended periods of time without fatigue	Nailing Techniques
The skill to fabricate and properly use templates	Building and Using Templates
The ability and knowledge necessary to obtain and maintain a well-stocked set of personal tools	Personal Tools

---

How Do You Set Up a Course Outline?

As we have seen, broad skill statements can be reduced to a few words which represent the titles of units of instruction to be used in a course outline. Any number of individual competencies which must be developed to demonstrate overall competency may ultimately be associated with each unit of instruction. This fact was discussed in Chapter 4, "Writing Competency Statements." The clusters of skills, which represent units of instruction, can be arranged into an outline for a competency-based instruction system.

The course outline that is used in a competency-based instruction system is somewhat different from a traditional one (see Illustration 12, pp. 42-43). The outlines for both the traditional and the competency-based system have some of the same general characteristics in that the units of instruction are logically arranged. The main difference between the conventional and performance-based course outline is that in the latter specific occupational competencies are associated with each unit of instruction and the order of their presentation has a functionally specific sequence. The rank ordering of competencies contributes to the instruction system's flexibility and allows for skill attainment to proceed naturally from the simple to the complex. The application of this central theory of the psychology of learning produces superior results.

One sample of a major unit of instruction for an automotive mechanics class, which contains several sets of competencies, is: "Internal Combusion Engines." Some competency tests which could be associated with this unit of instruction are:

> The student will record a minimum score of 90 percent on an objective examination related to the theory of internal combustion engines.

> The student will be able to identify, with 100 percent accuracy, all parts of the cutaway 6-cylinder internal combustion engine located in the classroom.

> The student will achieve a minimum performance rating of "4" (on a scale of 1-5) when demonstrating proficiency in tuning the live 8-cylinder engine located in the shop.

> The student will achieve a minimum performance rating of "4" (on a scale of 1-5) when demonstrating proficiency in troubleshooting a live internal combustion engine.

Two of the competency statements listed above contain testing standards for lower-order skills. One includes an objective test of the theory of internal combustion engines (*a*), and the other requires accurate identification of engine parts (*b*). These lower-order skills must be developed prior to moving on to higher-order proficiencies, because they constitute the basic knowledge which will be used in later tasks. Competency c, tuning the test engine, represents a higher-order set of skills and knowledge. Students must demonstrate expertise in tuning an 8-cylinder engine which is mounted on a static stand in the laboratory.

The highest-order set of skills and knowledge in this instructional unit is the ability to troubleshoot an automobile engine (d). This is a very complex procedure which requires a lot of skill and knowledge and which most students will develop only in the later, more advanced stages of the learning process.

The examples we have outlined emphasize the possibility that some units of instruction will contain basic, prerequisite skills and others very advanced skills. The instructional units of a competency-based curiculum should be sequenced progressively, so that the later units build on the skills taught in earlier segments. Educational psychologists have confirmed through years of research that the acquisition of skills and knowledge proceeds naturally from the simple to the complex. The negative effects of reversing this sequence have also been determined; that is, presenting too much new, unfamiliar, or complex information at one time creates confusion and hinders skill development. These points will be covered in greater detail in the last chapter of this book.

The instructor must devote considerable thought to the skill acquisition process when organizing the course outline, arranging units of instruction, and ordering the presentation of the skills which are associated with each unit. Basic units of instruction in a course outline for a competency-based instruction system should be organized following these general guidelines:

- Broad clusters of skills and knowledge (units of instruction) which are prerequisite should precede more advanced skills and knowledge.
- Units of instruction which do not have prerequisites should be grouped together in appropriate positions in the outline.
- The more advanced the broad skills or knowledge to be developed, the closer the unit of instruction associated with it should come to the end of the outline.

If these guidelines are followed, the result should be an outline arranged in a natural progression of difficulty from the simple to the complex.

DEVELOPMENTAL EXAMPLE: Part 6
Sequencing Unit Titles for the Course Outline

Examine the units of instruction that were identified for the job title of rough carpenter in our "Developmental Example." The titles of these units have been arranged in sequential order in accordance with the criteria listed above.

1. Safety on the Job
2. The Steel Tape Measure
3. Portable Power Tools
4. Measuring a Structure
5. Measuring and Cutting
6. Selecting Fasteners
7. Nailing Techniques
8. Fastening
9. Wood Identification
10. Wood Properties
11. Personal Tools
12. Maintaining Circular Saws
13. Maintaining Radial Arm Saws
14. Construction Mathematics
15. Using the Framing Square
16. Blueprint Reading
17. Estimating the Amount and Cost of Materials
18. Preparing Walls for Plastering
19. Constructing Handrails
20. Constructing Ladders
21. Building Trestles
22. Cost Control
23. Quality Control
24. Building and Using Templates
25. Bracing with Lumber
26. Bracing with Tie Rods and Anchor Bolts
27. Form Construction
28. Forming Footings
29. Forming Chutes
30. Constructing Walkways, Platforms, and Gangways
31. Cutting and Installing Subflooring
32. Troubleshooting Radial Arm Saws
33. Troubleshooting Circular Saws
34. Constructing Tunnel and Sewer Supports
35. Scaffold Construction
36. Sheathing
37. Plot Layout
38. Constructing Temporary Frame Shelters
39. Forming Concrete Piers
40. Forming Walls
41. Building and Inserting Window Bucks
42. Building and Inserting Door Bucks

The next step is to review the competency statements which were written for each unit of instruction (or cluster of skills and knowledge) and then rank order them within each unit by the level of difficulty. They are focal points around which lessons for skill development will be developed and, if reduced to a few words, can be used as lesson titles. The skills or knowledge taught in each lesson must be mastered before the student can be said to have successfully completed the unit of instruction.

An example of how this process works is provided in this sample from a basic electricity class. A broad set of skills or knowledge might read: "How to Calculate and Use Ohm's Law." The basic competencies for which the student will demonstrate proficiency are:

> The student will score a minimum of 100 percent on an objective examination consisting of 10 problems which require that students use the formula associated with Ohm's Law to find the value of *current*.

> The student will score a minimum of 100 percent on an objective examination consisting of 10 problems which require that students use Ohm's Law to find the various values of *resistance*.

> The student will score a minimum of 100 percent on an objective examination consisting of 10 problems which require that students use Ohm's Law to find the various values of *voltage*.

Each of these competency statements requires that certain values be accurately calculated using the Ohm's Law formula. These competencies can be condensed to become the titles of lessons. For example:

Lesson 22	Calculating Current
Lesson 23	Calculating Resistance
Lesson 24	Calculating Voltage

While preparing the course outline, the instructor must bear in mind that the competency statements themselves are descriptions of tests which specify a minimum acceptable score for skill attainment—they are *not* lesson titles or plans. However, by using lesson titles derived from these competency statements, the instructor will be well equipped to construct a comprehensive course outline. The lessons must be carefully sequenced under each broad unit title. This special sequence is the essence of the competency-based system. It can be thought of as a road map of specific learning activities which leads to the achievement of prestated goals.

DEVELOPMENTAL EXAMPLE: Part 7
Selecting Lesson Titles for the Course Outline

Now we will again refer to our "Developmental Example" and select that portion of the course outline dealing with the use of power tools. An appropriate title for the unit of instruction based on this broad cluster of skills and knowledge is: "Power Tools." Subunits could then deal with the competencies associated with each tool—the circular saw, the electric drill, the saber saw, the electric plane, the radial arm saw. Several lesson titles must then be chosen for each tool. Each of these titles should relate to a competency (or competencies) needed for general proficiency in the use of the tool. All of the lessons must be completed before the student is considered to have finished the unit successfully.

Recall the competency statements associated with the use of the circular saw as listed in Chapter 4:

1. The student will achieve a minimum performance rating of "5" (on a scale of 1-5) when demonstrating the safe use of the circular saw.
2. The student will demonstrate skill in using the circular saw to make bevel cuts which will join with an opening of less than 1/16th of an inch.
3. The student will demonstrate skill in making a freehand cut along a predetermined line with the circular saw with 100 percent accuracy.
4. The student will make 10 rip cuts with the circular saw on various types of lumber to within 1/32nd of an inch of the dimensions specified by the instructor.
5. The student will make 10 crosscuts with the circular saw on various types of lumber to within 1/32nd of an inch of the dimensions specified by the instructor.
6. The student will achieve a minimum performance rating of "4" (on a scale of 1-5) when demonstrating the use of the circular saw on five advanced construction projects as specified by the instructor.

Each of these competency statements can be reduced to a few words to create lesson titles. The arrangement of these lessons should proceed from the simple to the complex, and follow a natural progression based on the attainment of prerequisite skills followed by higher-level tasks which build on the use of these basics.

Lesson 1	Safe Use of the Circular Saw
Lesson 2	Making Crosscuts
Lesson 3	Making Rip Cuts
Lesson 4	Making Bevel Cuts
Lesson 5	Making Freehand Cuts
Lesson 6	Projects

Now let's examine how the lessons for another broad set of knowledge related to the use of the framing square might be arranged. The
broad cluster of knowledge reads: "The ability to use the framing
square." The title of the unit of instruction might be: "Using the
Framing Square."
The competency statements which are associated with demonstrating proficiency in using the framing square might read as follows:

1. The student will score a minimum of 100 percent on an
   objective examination relating to the nomenclature of the
   framing square.
2. The student will score a minimum of 100 percent accuracy
   when demonstrating proficiency in using the hundredths
   scale to convert 5 separate hundredths lengths to sixteenths.
3. The student will achieve a minimum performance rating of
   "4" (on a scale of 1-5) when demonstrating proficiency in
   using the octagon table of the framing square to convert a
   four-sided timber to an eight-sided one.
4. The student will score 100 percent on an examination requiring the use of the Essex board measure feature of the
   framing square to determine board feet.
5. The student will achieve a minimum score of 100 percent
   when demonstrating skill in reading the brace table of the
   framing square.

Each of the foregoing competency statements can now be reduced
and converted to the titles of lessons. The title possibilities are:

Lesson 1	Framing Square Nomenclature
Lesson 2	The Hundredths Scale
Lesson 3	The Octagon Scale
Lesson 4	Essex Board Measure
Lesson 5	Brace Measure

After completing the course outline, the next task in the development of a competency-based instruction system is the planning of
learning activities that the students must participate in as part of each
lesson in order to attain the knowledge and skills that have been outlined. The writer of a competency-based instruction system must carefully specify and sequence the tasks which the student must perform
in order to develop skills and knowledge to a point where competency
testing can appropriately take place.

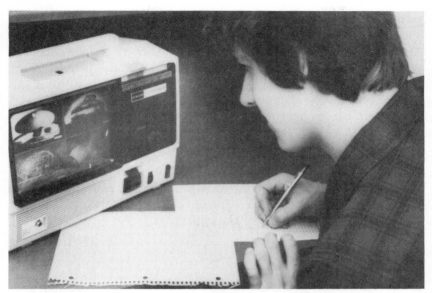

Illustration 21. The success of individualized instruction depends largely on the careful organization of learning activities.

How Do You Develop Organized Learning Activities?

You have already learned that one of the characteristics of a competency-based instruction system is that it is individualized. Within such a system students should be able to work on the development of prestated skills and knowledge at their own rate of learning because of its flexibility. The way in which this instructional system is arranged makes it possible, theoretically, for 20 students to be working on as many different lessons. At the heart of the competency-based instruction system is the manner in which learning activities for the development of competencies are derived and managed by the instructor. We will now examine the scope of the competency-based cycle and various methods and techniques which will assist in the development of learning activities for competency lessons. They are:

> Components of the Competency-Based Instruction Cycle
>
> Developing Learning Activities Packages
>
> Writing Programmed Learning Activities Sheets
>
> Developing Work Station Learning Activities

Components of the Competency-Based Instruction Cycle

A student may be engaged in any one of the five general phases of purposeful learning activity which make up the competency-based instruction cycle. The five levels of learning activity in which a student may be involved are:

1. Identification of the skill to be learned
2. Familiarization with the skill
3. Development of the skill
4. Testing of skill attainment
5. Evaluation of the results

The instructor's job in a competency-based instruction system is to manage all purposeful learning activity so that each student is in an appropriate phase of the skills acquisition cycle at all times. The instructor must by necessity be aware of the relative progress of each student within the sequence of learning activities. The instructor must also know exactly where each student is in the sequence of activities and what skill they are attempting to develop.

1. *Identification of the skill to be learned.* The introductory part of each lesson is the presentation or acquaintance phase of instruction for the skill or knowledge to be acquired. In this initial stage, the purpose of the lesson and its nature must be conveyed to the student, and the actual specification of the competency which is to be attained should be stated. Once the student knows what it is that the lesson is designed to accomplish, the second phase can be initiated.

2. *Familiarization with the skill.* The student can read about the skill from a book or other printed material, view a slide-tape series or other audiovisual material, the instructor can demonstrate the skill and give a brief lecture, or combine any of these learning activities to encourage the development of the skill that has been identified in phase one. Demonstrations of the refined motions and techniques associated with a skill are often appropriate at this point in the cycle. The purpose of the second phase of instruction in the competency-based system is to give the student a mental image of what is to be accomplished as preparation for the next step in the skill learning process.

3. *Development of the skill.* The third step is the actual process of developing the skill or knowledge which has been selected. This is

where hands-on instruction begins. The instructor, in most cases, should be aware of the precise moment at which a student enters this stage of competency learning. It is important that the student who is attempting to learn critical skills (such as striking a welding torch) be supervised by the instructor. Safety procedures must be observed and the student's first practice attempts should be guided. A workbook exercise or question-and-answer sheet can be used if theory knowledge, rather than a hands-on skill, is being developed for competency attainment.

The development of skill proficiency is a very important phase of the learning progression. The student should have every opportunity to compare the results of attempts at demonstrating skill attainment with a good example. The instructor should provide as much positive feedback and encouragement to the students as possible. The student should have the freedom to advance through attempts at mastery until the skill to be developed becomes second nature.

4. *Testing of skill attainment.* The fourth stage in competency development is a demonstration that the specified competency level has been achieved as shown by the student's performance on a skill test. This is the first time during the learning sequence that the student actually attempts to attain the competency ratings that are listed for a particular unit of instruction. This attempt should be scheduled, managed, and observed by the instructor.

5. *Evaluation of the result.* The results of the learner's attempt to meet a specified competency should be carefully evaluated against the prestated performance goal in the fifth phase of the competency learning cycle. Student performance should be compared with the standard given in the competency statement. The results of the attempt at skill mastery should then be evaluated by the instructor and explained to the student. If required, suggestions for further practice, or methods for improving performance, should be pointed out to the student. The student either will be instructed to repeat the cycle of learning activities so that additional competency can be built or will be credited with successful skill attainment and directed to move on to the next step of competency development within the job title curriculum.

The instructor should be aware of the lesson or learning activity each student is working on. Managing student progress through the five phases of the development cycle is possible in a competency-based instruction system because of the specially sequenced course outline and the careful selection of organized learning activities for each step. These activities can include Learning Activities Packages, Programmed Learning Sheets and work station activities.

Developing Learning Activities Packages

Learning Activities Packages (or LAPs) are a means of imparting skills and knowledge using methods and techniques which are very compatible with a competency-based instruction system. LAPs are instructional modules which can be used very effectively to introduce new skills and knowledge to students—the first step in the skills acquisition process. Learning Activities Packages are guides for the orderly progression of instruction. They also assist the instructor in managing the learning process by allowing for independent work by the student within a framework provided by the instructor.

LAPs encourage students to work at their own pace. A LAP ideally states the goals, and includes activities and exercises to insure that the student is able to begin an orderly development of skill proficiency. The following are characteristics of effective Learning Activities Packages:

- A LAP is a well-coordinated instructional module which is written in goal-oriented terms.
- A LAP deals with just one central concept or unit of instruction.
- A LAP allows students to work at their own pace.
- A LAP is generally teacher constructed, but may sometimes be purchased commercially.
- The scope of a LAP may vary.
- The LAP releases the instructor from many routine tasks related to assigning work and allows the instructor to work individually with students who may be experiencing difficulty.
- A LAP can either supplement or constitute an actual lesson within a competency sequence.
- LAPs are specially sequenced.

The Learning Activities Package is an ideal learning device to use in the earlier stages of instruction. Let's examine the general components of a Learning Activities Package. For your reference, a sample of a LAP for a typing class is shown in Illustration 22.

Identification Markings. Various kinds of identification should be incorporated into each LAP. This set of information should include the student's name, the date, and the title of the unit of instruction taken from the outline. One of the best methods of identifying Learning Activities Packages is to adopt the same numbering system used in sequencing the course outline for the competency-based instruction system. For example, "Learning Activities Package II-3" would correspond to the third lesson of the second unit of instruction in the outline.

Competencies to be acquired. There should be a statement at the beginning of each LAP which specifies the competency which the package is designed to develop. There could, for example, be four LAPs associated with the development of one competency, or more than one competency could be developed in one LAP. It is of vital importance to a competency-based instruction system that the student know from the outset precisely what is to be accomplished by following the directions of the LAPs. The answer to the all-important question asked by every student—"What do I have to learn?"—is supplied when the competency to be mastered is clearly identified at the beginning of the LAPs.

Instructional Materials Needed. A complete list of the instructional materials needed by the student to complete the activities module should be contained in the LAP. The student might, for example, need a book on basic carpentry, a protractor, and a framing square to begin work on a particular LAP. All of the materials and resources which are going to be needed by students to complete the LAP must be specified.

List Specific Learning Activities. The activities in the LAP should be presented sequentially so that the student is guided logically through the learning process. Students should be alerted to stumbling blocks that they might encounter in their efforts to complete the exercise. Adequate pauses should be written into the LAP so that the student can receive feedback at the appropriate stages in the learning sequence.

Conclusion. There should be instructions in the LAP that tell the student what to do with the completed LAP and how to proceed from that point. The instructor should set up specific instructions at the end of each LAP as an aid in managing competency-based instruction.

LEARNING ACTIVITIES PACKAGE
TYPING I

A. _____ _____
   DATE   STUDENT NAME

TITLE: Learning to Set and Clear Tab Stops

IDENTIFICATION: Section III-4

B.   *Competencies to be met:*

1. The student will set five tab stops in less than 30 seconds using margin settings supplied by the instructor.
2. The student will achieve a minimum performance rating of "3" when demonstrating proficiency in using the "sweep clear" feature of the IBM Selectric Typewriter.
3. The student will produce one mailable copy of the "Columnar Tabulation Problem" (Handout #14-7) in less than five minutes.
4. The student will type an errorless copy of "Wilson Tabulation Problem #5" in one minute or less.

C.   *Instructional materials needed:*

1. Typing paper
2. Typing eraser
3. Handout #14-6: "The Purpose of Tabulation"
4. Your *ABC Typing* book
5. The operator's manual for your typewriter
6. Handout #14-7: "Columnar Tabulation Problem"
7. Handout #14-8: "Wilson Tabulation Problems"

D.   *Specific learning activities:*

1. Read handout 14-6, "Purpose of Tabulation."
2. Complete Tabulation Problem #1 in your *ABC Typing* book, page 48.

3. Call on your instructor if you experience difficulty.

4. Complete tabulation problem #2 in your *ABC Typing* book, page 48.

5. Read the operator's manual, pages 15-16, on how to use the "sweep clear" feature on your typewriter.

6. Enter tab stops at 10, 30, 50 and 60. Check to see if they are set properly by striking the tab key and reading the margin scale.

7. Clear the tab stops you set in step number 6 by using the "sweep clear" feature on your typewriter.

8. Test to see if the tab stops have been cleared. If not, reread pages 15-16 of the operator's manual and return to step 5. If your tabs have been cleared proceed to step 9.

9. Read handout #14-7, "Columnar Tabulation Problems."

10. Use your copy of the "Wilson Tabulation Problems" (Handout #14-8). Follow the sequence of activities listed below for tabulation problems 1-5.

   a. Set your tabs.
   b. Test to see if they are set; type the problem.
   c. Use the "sweep clear" feature to clear tabs.
   d. Test to see if they are clear.

   If you experience any difficulty call on your instructor; othwise proceed to step 11.

11. Read the tabulation problem on page 104 of your *ABC Typing* book. Call on your instructor to time your typing exercise. Correct any errors that you make, but attempt to type the tabulation exercise without errors.

E. *Conclusion*

   Call upon your instructor to verify your assessment of your skill development at this stage. The instructor should tell you at this point if you are ready to proceed with competency testing or need more skill development.

Illustration 22. Sample Learning Activities Package.

PROGRAMMED LEARNING ACTIVITIES SHEET
PLUMBING

DATE   STUDENT NAME

TITLE: **Learning to Unclog Drains**
IDENTIFICATION: **Unit IV-6**

Competency statement:

The student will achieve a minimum performance rating of "3" when demonstrating proficiency in unclogging various types of drains.

General information:

Drains may become clogged by solid wastes. The common plunger can be used in a first attempt to unclog a drain. If this fails, removing the fixture trap plug is the next step in the process of unclogging a drain.

If removing the trap plug does not result in the successful opening of the drain, the obstruction is located in another section of the pipe. The next step is the use of the snake. There are as many different variations for unclogging a drain as there are fixtures and function (i.e., unclogging a bathtub drain, lavatory, toilet, sink, etc.). The same basic procedures apply in each case.

STEP 1—*Write your answer to the following questions in the space that is provided.*

1. What tool might the plumber use first to attempt to unclog a drain?
   _____ (Write in your answer)
2. A plumber may choose to use a snake after performing what procedure and not succeeding?
   _____ (Write in your answer)
3. Is there more than one type of drain?
   _____ (Write in your answer)

You may check the accuracy of your answer by turning the page upside down and reading the key.

STEP 2—*The Plunger*

The common plunger can be used in a first attempt to unclog a drain. Follow these steps: (*a*) fill the collection bowl with water, (*b*) vigorously work the plunger up and down and attempt to free the obstruction, (*c*) observe the water level.

Did the water level recede? If so, you have unclogged the drain. If not, proceed to Step 3.

STEP 3—*Removal of the Fixture Trap*

A trap is a bend in the pipe which fills with water to create a seal which prevents harmful sewer gases from escaping. Traps often have a trap plug which can be removed to facilitate the removal of obstructions which commonly occur in or near the trap. Our lab model does have a trap plug.

Procedures:

1. Take a container and place it under the trap plug to catch water which will run out when you remove it.
2. Remove the trap plug and washer and use a narrow screwdriver to clear out any obstructions.
3. Replace the washer and trap plug.
4. Fill the bowl from which the drain empties and observe the water level.

Does the fixture bowl drain properly? If the answer to the question is "no," you have not been successful and must proceed to Step 4.

Step 4 and following steps are not shown in this sample.

KEY: (1) Plunger (2) Removing the trap plug (3) Yes

Illustration 23. Sample Programmed Learning Activities Sheet.

Developing Programmed Learning Activities Sheets

A Programmed Learning Activities Sheet is similar to a Learning Activities Package, but it focuses on a single procedure which is to be developed by the student step by step. A Learning Activities Package, on the other hand, may have a broader scope. The purpose of the Programmed Learning Activities Sheet is to impart specific procedural knowledge or skill to students in a *self-contained instructional unit*. A sample of a Programmed Learning Activities Sheet for a plumbing course is shown in Illustration 23. Notice that this Programmed Learning Activities Sheet is self-contained and does not depend on outside printed learning resources.

Another feature of the Programmed Learning Activities Sheet is that it supplies the student with the answer to the problem (immediate feedback) after each stage in the step-by-step progression. The specific activity of the student is controlled through instructions given on the sheet and timely reinforcement of learning takes place on an individual basis.

Programmed Learning Activities Sheets have these characteristics:

- They state in specific terms what the student will accomplish as a result of completing the activity.
- They utilize a step-by-step progression of programmed learning activities.
- They require an immediate student response.
- They allow for the immediate checking of the results by the student.
- They are self-contained and have enough information in them to constitute a complete lesson.

Developing Work Station Learning Activities

This is another method of skills instruction which is highly compatible with a competency-based system. This approach is also student centered, but in this case students interact in a true-to-life work station until skill mastery is achieved. Certain types of occupational skills are particularly suited to hands-on activities. Work stations give the students an opportunity to apply their recently acquired knowledge and level of skill achievement in a realistic practice situation.

Now we will return to the ''Developmental Example'' and use as our focal point one of the more advanced skills from the course outline for the job title of rough carpenter—"Cutting and Installing Subfloors." This example will illustrate how a work station simulation can be used. A Learning Activities Package and a Programmed Learning Activities Sheet are referred to in this section of the "Developmental Example" to show how both might be used in conjunction with a work station simulation.

Illustration 24. Many occupational programs use work stations as a vital part of their instructional activities.

DEVELOPMENTAL EXAMPLE: Part 8
Work Station Simulation Activity

TITLE: Cutting and Installing Subfloors
LOCATION: Parking Lot

COMPETENCY STATEMENT: The student will achieve a minimum performance rating of "4" (on a scale of 1-5) when demonstrating proficiency in constructing and installing a subfloor for a residence to the dimensions specified by the instructor.

INTRODUCTION: Assume that you are working for a residential construction contractor as a rough carpenter. The task that you have been assigned to do is to cut and install a subfloor for a residence. You are to use the instructions which are provided at this work station and install a subfloor on the parking lot which conforms to the exact dimensions specified by the instructor. You should feel complete responsibility for this task as if you were actually employed. You are expected to perform this task at a level of competence sufficient to insure your continued employment with the contractor.

INSTRUCTIONS:

1. Review the Learning Activities Package associated with subfloors (IV-9). This will reacquaint you with the necessary steps that you must follow in installing a subfloor.
2. Complete Programed Learning Activities Sheet #50 on how to interpret and calculate plans and measurements on materials for the installation of a subfloor.
3. Open the directions envelope for this work station and begin.

The instructor in this "Developmental Example" has predetermined through the use of the "Directions Envelope" the activities that the student at the work station will be involved in. This controls or programs the learning situation. The instructor, as learning manager, is thus more able to check on the progress of the student and control the sequence of instruction and learning activities when the student is working on an advanced project.

One of the most useful features of the work station simulation concept is that the student is confronted with a realistic set of employment-related circumstances. This requires a thorough integration of the skills and knowledge which have been acquired.

Work station learning activities offer the following advantages for developing competency:

- Work station simulations are realistic and represent conditions students will encounter on the job.
- The instructor can efficiently provide input related to a broad range of competencies through a work station simulation.
- Work station simulations allow instructors to present the student with varied programed learning situations.
- Work station simulations are normally associated with the more advanced stages of skill learning and call for the integration of previously learned skills and knowledge.
- Work station simulations provide for student-based decision making with immediate feedback as to the results of student action.
- Both Learning Activities Packages and Programmed Learning Activities Sheets can be used with station simulators.

Work station simulations can be used in all types of vocational-technical instruction, but they are most compatible with a system that concentrates on the development of prestated competencies.

REVIEW QUESTIONS

1. How can the writer of a competency-based curriculum identify the units of instruction for a course outline?

2. What is the main difference between a traditional course outline and one for a competency-based instruction system?

3. What criteria could be used to put the competency presentations in sequence?

4. How can the writer of a competency-based curriculum determine relevant lesson titles?

5. Why must organized learning activities be developed for each of the lessons in a competency-based instruction system?

6. List the components of the competency-based instruction system.

7. What is a Learning Activities Package?

8. What are some of the unique characteristics of Learning Activities Packages?

9. What is a Programmed Learning Activities Sheet?

10. How do the characteristics of work station learning activities promote occupational skills acquisition?

CHAPTER

Competency-Based
Evaluation
and
Recordkeeping

SIX

T HERE is a difference in the meanings of the words *testing, evaluation,* and *grading.* These differences should be acknowledged and understood by an instructor who is converting to a competency-based curriculum.

A *test,* or competency requirement, is an instrument, device, or hands-on task that can be used to measure the degree of student success in relation to prestated performance standards.

Evaluation is the act of assessing the results of student performance on these tests relative to the prestated goals. Evaluation is a method through which the instructor can determine how effective the competency-based instruction system has been in helping the individual student gain knowledge and skills. Evaluation in a competency-based instruction system is also used to determine the relative rate of student progress with respect to the overall objectives. The instructor can then make intelligent choices as to what specific competencies the students should be pursuing.

For our purposes, the word *grading* refers to the process of assigning a symbolic label to accumulated evaluations of student performance at specified times. The appropriateness of using grades with a competency-based instruction system is highly questionable. For this reason, grading will not be considered an effective part of competency evaluation. However, a separate section of this chapter is devoted to a discussion of some alternatives that an instructor can use if the school system requires that grade assignments be made.

Competency-Based Evaluation

There are four stages associated with evaluation in a competency-based instruction system. They are illustrated and discussed below.

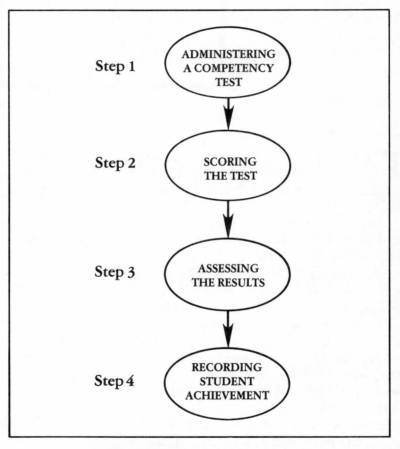

Illustration 25. Competency Evaluation

Step 1, *administering a competency test,* may involve a demonstration of a hands-on skill or the taking of a paper-and-pencil test.

Step 2, *scoring the test*, requires an assessment of the students' attempt to demonstrate competency attainment. This phase of competency evaluation consists of tallying up the correct responses or scoring student performance and assigning a score based on a rating scale set up for the specific competency which has been observed.

Step 3, *assessing the results*, is the instructor's evaluation of student performance with respect to the overall objectives and relative student progress.

Step 4, *recording student achievement*, generally refers to a tabulation of the results of the evaluation on a form which can be used as a record of student competency attainment.

Most of the measurements and evaluations which are made in competency-based instruction are based on systems developed by the instructor. The instructor either rates the observed student behavior using a rating scale, or constructs written exams for measuring cognitive knowledge. An individual who is designing a competency-based instruction system must develop skill and expertise in organizing and scoring competency performance tests, in the construction of written exams, and in using various techniques of evaluation. The tests of student performance and rating scales which are developed by an instructor directly influence the quality of evaluation. An instructor who is planning to convert to a system of instruction which focuses on prestated goals must understand and use sound methods of administering and scoring tests.

Some concepts which may help instructors test and evaluate student performance in a fair and objective manner will be examined in this chapter. They include:

> Characteristics of an Effective Evaluation System
>
> Competency Testing Techniques
>
> Competency Recordkeeping
>
> Grading in a Competency-Based Instruction System

Characteristics of an Effective Evaluation System

The purpose of an evaluation system is to accurately assess student performance in relation to prestated goals. The characteristics of an effective evaluation system for a competency-based instruction system are that it:

Be fair and impartial
Measure only what has been presented to the student
Use sound principles of test construction
Be valid
Be reliable
Be objective
Be comprehensive
Be discriminating
Be systematic and continuous

Each of the characteristics of an evaluation program will be briefly examined.

Be fair and impartial. Most instructors strive to make every component of their evaluation system as fair as possible. The fact that an effective evaluation system is *fair* and *impartial* underscores the need for diligence in maintaining high standards in the evaluation of student performance. The instructor must be able to evaluate the performance of different students in a consistent manner. This is true for both performance tests, which are most common in competency-based programs, and paper-and-pencil tests.

If a student whose performance is being measured, for example, was involved in a serious infraction of shop rules in the past this should not influence the performance rating on a particular skill which is currently being tested. There may, however, be other areas of competency under which the student's improper behavior could be noted in the evaluation process, for example, work attitudes or shop safety. The instructor should strive to exclude as much bias as possible in the scoring and evaluation of student performance.

The elements of fairness and impartiality can be enhanced when rating student performance if it is possible to involve more than one person in the evaluation or scoring. The degree of fairness can also be increased by narrowing the observation strictly to the activity or topic that is specified in the competency statement. Ideally, the precise characteristics required for competency should be ''checked-off'' while observing student performance.

Measure only what has been presented to the student. A competency-based instruction system should be designed so that the prerequisites or simpler skills and knowledge that the student must master are presented before the more complex skills are introduced. The testing and evaluation sequence should parallel the instructional sequence that each student is following. The rating instrument or test used should only test what has been presented to the student in preparatory materials and activities or in previous units. An inaccurate assessment of whether a student is succeeding in an occupational instruction program would be made if more knowledge and skill than the student has had an opportunity to master is included in the test.

Consider the following example of how a test might produce inaccurate readings of student performance. Assume that a student in a carpentry program has just completed a basic unit of instruction on the use of the transit. If, after completing this introductory unit, a student was required to lay out a residential building site, valid results that would be useful in the overall evaluation process would not be obtained. The student might be able to demonstrate basic competency in setting up and using the transit but this student most probably would not be able to lay out a building site until more advanced skills and knowledge could be gained.

Use sound principles of test construction. There are entire courses of study which are designed to teach individuals how to construct valid and reliable written tests. The process of designing a good examination is time consuming and far more difficult a task than that which the students face in preparing for the same examination. An instructor who is preparing paper-and-pencil tests for measuring cognitive knowledge attainment should apply only those basic principles of test construction which have been shown to be sound and effective. Some of these principles are examined in detail later in this chapter.

Be valid. All aspects of the evaluation process in competency-based instruction systems must be valid. The term *valid* implies that the evaluation instrument or testing situation measures what it is supposed to measure. Any evaluation technique used in a competency-based instruction system is valid only to the extent that it accurately measures and subsequently assesses the attainment of the prestated skills and knowledge.

Several approaches can be used to enhance the validity of evaluation in a competency-based system: (1) Involve advisory committees in the construction and revision of competency tests. (2) To determine the appropriateness of current occupational competency requirements, evaluate the performance of former students by interviewing their employers. Revise your standards accordingly. (3) When determining the validity of the evaluation program, involve as many of your colleagues as possible in the assessment process.

Be reliable. Another characteristic of a sound evaluation program for a competency-based system is that it is reliable. The term *reliable* means that under similar circumstances the same results would be obtained by another evaluator with a similar group of students. Reliability is also demonstrated if one obtains the same results on a written examination given to similar groups of students. This term applies to being consistent when observing, rating, and evaluating hands-on performance tests.

Be objective. The more objective an evaluation system becomes, the less the chance that the personal bias of the evaluator will enter into the evaluation process. Objectivity in a competency-based instruction system should be extremely high because it uses distinct and precise prestated competency requirements.

Be comprehensive. The term *comprehensive* indicates that student knowledge or skill attainment is tested and evaluated very thoroughly. Literally all elements of the skill or knowledge to be developed are measured and evaluated. A competency-based evaluation system would be less than desirable if it failed to measure any aspect of the skills and knowledge needed for the student to be employable.

Be discriminating. The characteristic of comprehensiveness is closely related to how discriminating the evaluation instrument or performance test is. An evaluation system which is discriminating can be used to discern small differences in student peformance. The type of evaluation system which is produced when using a competency-based curriculum is detailed and discriminating by nature. This is one of the advantages in using a competency-based system of instruction. The instructor must be able to determine which students have met minimum employability standards as opposed to those who might have fallen short of or even exceeded the prestated performance goal.

Be systematic and continuous. The components of an evaluation system for a competency-based curriculum should be systematically applied. The testing and evaluation cycle begins only after the students have been given a clear statement of the skill or knowledge that is desired and how they will be tested, have been presented with appropriate instructional information, and have had sufficient time in which to develop competency in the specified area. The entire curriculum is also systematic in that it proceeds from the simple to the complex.

The evaluation that takes place must also be continuous. The instructor must vigorously pursue routine evaluation of student performance on a minute-by-minute basis. Very little could prove to be more disastrous in a competency-based instruction system than intermittent evaluation. Students must have immediate feedback regarding the results of their attempts at skill mastery if they are to engage in purposeful learning activities.

Competency-Based Testing Techniques

Two basic types of evaluation can take place in a competency-based instruction system. One is objective and the other is subjective. You should recall from Chapter Four, where competency statements were being written, that basically there are also only two types of performance measures: objective and subjective.

Objective Tests

Objective testing for the evaluation of skill and knowledge acquisition can be accomplished either through direct objective measures (actual measurements taken using various devices) or through objective testing with a written exam.

Direct objective measures require that an actual physical measurement be made of student performance. For example, a direct objective measure is included in the following competency statement.

> The student will demonstrate proficiency in laying a row of bricks which are verified as being accurately placed by using a builder's level.

The builder's level in this example is the instrument that is being used to make a direct objective measure of competency attainment because this particular device accurately measures the levelness of a flat surface, in this case the row of bricks.

Other instruments which can be used to make direct objective measures are stopwatches, rulers, tapes, micrometers, measuring cups, thermometers, scales, and those manufacturer's specifications that can be quantified and measured. Direct objective measures are normally associated with performance-based, hands-on skills.

Objective testing with a paper-and-pencil exam is generally only applicable for measuring cognitive knowledge attainment. The number of written examinations which are required in a program, however, will vary according to the subject matter. For example, there would be a significant number of written exams associated with a course for a bookkeeper. There would be correspondingly few written tests used in a masonry program.

Writers of competency-based instruction programs will discover quickly that most of the tests to be used must be specially designed for a specific program. Few commercially-prepared exams are readily available for measuring knowledge attainment for specific, and sometimes localized, job title competencies. The importance of following acceptable principles of test construction cannot be overemphasized. An instructor who is writing test items for competency evaluation should be familiar with the proper techniques used in writing test items. The validity of the test (the importance of which we have already expressed) is enhanced by using the proper techniques.

Five basic types of written test items commonly used in teacher-made tests are:

> Essay questions
> Short answer questions
> Multiple choice questions
> Matching problems
> True-false questions

Essay Questions. Essay questions are one of the oldest types of test items and should be reserved primarily for testing the integration of advanced cognitive knowledge. Some principles used in constructing essay questions follow:

- Use essay questions to test mastery of complex principles and processes.
- In order to be as objective as possible, define the type of answer that is required within the question.
- Provide adequate time for the student to respond when tested.
- Use an analytical scoring technique.

The following example is a sample of an essay question for our "Developmental Example."

What are the steps to be followed when doing a plot layout for a residential structure? Discuss each.

The nature of the response required for this question is complex. The student must give considerable thought to the response. The instructor is testing the student's ability to integrate and interpret a broad range of knowledge.

Analytical scoring of essay questions is recommended for a competency-based instruction system. The reason will become apparent when the technique is described. Analytical scoring of an essay question involves weighting certain desired responses and scoring the student's answer to the essay question in relation to how many of the required elements are included in the answer. If the answers to the question in our example were scored analytically, each major step in determining a plot layout would carry a certain weight.

Short Answer Questions. This type of test item is frequently used by instructors. It should be of limited use in a competency-based system since it is used primarily for measuring outcomes in the early stages of learning. It is better suited for measuring the retention of facts than of concepts. Since a student must respond with a relatively short answer, the major concern associated with its use is the proper phrasing of the question. The use of short answer questions should conform to the following principles:

- Questions should be constructed to elicit only one response.
- Questions should be direct whenever possible
- The proper answer should be clearly identifiable with the question
- The blank or space for response should ideally come at the end of the question.

Several examples of short answer test items which are associated with our "Developmental Example" follow:

1. What is the equivalent measure of 8/32nds of an inch in sixteenths?
2. What is the area of a structure which measures 65 feet × 108 feet?
3. How many degrees are there in a right angle?

Multiple-Choice Questions. This kind of test item has two main parts. The statement which precedes the choices for the response is known as the *stem*. The *response section* is the second part of a multiple choice question and contains the correct answer and the distractors, or incorrect responses. The student's task on a multiple-choice test is to select the best answer to the question which is posed in the stem and to indicate the chosen response in a manner which is spelled out in the directions of the question.

A properly written multiple-choice test item discriminates between levels of performance. The reader should recall that this characteristic is desirable in the overall evaluation program for a competency-based instruction system. Some general principles of writing multiple-choice test items are:

- Write the test item so that it is as discriminating as possible.
- Present only one question or problem to be solved in the stem.
- Phrase the correct response so that it is clearly correct.
- Phrase the stem of the multiple choice question in positive terms.
- Emphasize negative responses by underlining and putting the negative word in capital letters when they must be included.
- All responses should be in grammatical agreement and parallel construction should be used.
- Distractors, or incorrect responses, should relate to the proper response and seem plausible but be incorrect; be a common error which is made by learners who have not yet reached mastery; or be a statement which is accurate in content but does not answer the question.

A test item should be constructed so that it measures an objective which has been prestated by the instructor. A multiple-choice test item should be written so that the student who has not yet mastered a particular set of knowledge will experience difficulty in answering the question. Remember that the purpose of testing is to evaluate whether or not the desired level of mastery has been achieved. A majority of the students who have achieved mastery in a particular area should experience little difficulty in answering a well constructed multiple-choice test item.

An instructor who is writing a multiple-choice test question should focus on a single item or piece of knowledge to be tested. A good method of checking to see if this standard can be met is to see whether the test question could be answered without the list of responses.

The following multiple-choice test question could be used in our rough carpentry curriculum:

Which one of the following statements adequately defines the word *span*?

a) It is the distance from the top of the roof to the plate.
b) It is the vertical distance from the top of the plate to the center line of the ridge.
c) It is the distance between two opposite walls.
d) It is the distance between the outside corner plate to the ridge board.

Matching Problems. This type of test item is very similar to the multiple-choice question. It is different in that a series of stems are offered in one column and a series of responses are listed in the other column. The student must match each response with the proper stem. The following are general principles for writing matching problems:

- All responses must be plausible.
- A matching test section should be homogeneous, that is, related to one particular topic.
- Use a larger or smaller number of responses than stems.
- Indicate in the instructions whether a response can be used more than once.

An example of a matching problem for our "Developmental Example" is shown below:

Read the definitions in the right-hand column. Place the letter of the definition which matches the proper word in the left-hand column in the space provided to the left. No response can be used more than once.

_____ 1. The Gable Roof	a. shortened common rafters
	b. rafters which extend from the hip to valley rafters
_____ 2. Hip roof	
	c. the simplest of the pitched roofs
_____ 3. Cripple Jacks	
	d. the ends of the gable roofs sliced diagonally
_____ 4. Jack Rafters	
	e. butt hips

True-False Questions. True-false test questions are very difficult to construct properly. They have the lowest reliability rating of all the types of test items. They normally consist of a statement which the student must read and evaluate in light of whether or not the student believes that the statement is true or false. Principles that should be followed when writing true-false test items are:

- Each statement should relate to only one idea or concept.
- The question should be written so that a properly prepared student instantly recognizes it as true or false.
- Rarely use negative statements and avoid double negatives.
- Do not use words such as *always, never, none, all, etc.*

The following are typical examples of true-false test items that might be used in a carpentry class.

Place a "T" in the space to the left of each statement if that statement is true or an "F" if it is false.

_____   1. Perimeter insulation is installed where the slab meets the foundation wall.
_____   2. Forms are needed to construct block walls.
_____   3. Steps should be anchored to the main structure.

The acquisition of skills and knowledge necessary for employment is the purpose of occupational instruction. Determining whether or not a student has attained an appropriate level of skill is the purpose of evaluation in a competency-based instruction system.

Subjective Evaluation Techniques.

Many of the areas in which a student must demonstrate proficiency can only be evaluated through subjective means. The instructor must observe student performance and literally pass judgment on whether or not the quality of performance meets the standards of employability. This type of subjective scoring is quite typical of occupational instruction. In this section we will discuss how an instructor in a competency-based instruction system can score and evaluate fairly using subjective evaluation techniques.

A common technique associated with subjective competency evaluation is *rating*. Rating generally involves the use of some type of scale on which observed student performance can be ranked. The three types of rating systems which we will discuss are:

Adjective rating scales
Numerical rating scales
Graphic rating scales

Adjective Rating Scale. This type of rating system uses words, particularly descriptive adjectives, to describe the quality of student performance. One of the most common is the rating scale which uses terms similar to:

_____	Superior
_____	Excellent
_____	Good
_____	Fair
_____	Poor

This type of rating scale is somewhat flexible because the instructor can use a sliding scale of meanings or definitions to suit different sets of circumstances. There are inherent disadvantages with this type of rating scale, however, in that each of the words, such as *excellent*, can mean one thing to the evaluator and another to the student-learner.

An instructor who uses an adjective rating scale should specify and possibly demonstrate the kind of behavior needed to achieve the required rating. This technique will increase the fairness and objectivity of the system.

Numerical Rating Scales. This kind of rating scale uses numbers to express the measurement of degrees of student performance. The number of points on a rating scale can vary but usually it is an odd number so that the midpoint of the scale may be equated with average performance.

The numerical rating scale shown here can be used to measure student performance by marking a position along the scale which corresponds to the degree of student performance. The high end of the scale is normally associated with superior performance and the lower end correspondingly with poor performance.

1	2	3	4	5

Graphic Rating Scales. This type of rating system makes use of both the adjective rating scale and the numerical scale. It is more valid and reliable because descriptive phrases relating to student behavior and relative numerical marking are considered concurrently. A graphic evaluation scale which includes a five-point rating scale could be used in a competency-based instruction system. An example that is particularly useful in a performance-based system of instruction is:

5 Indicates superior mastery of an occupational competency
4 Indicates better than average mastery of an occupational competency
3 Indicates minimum acceptable performance to maintain employment
2 Indicates below average mastery of the competency
1 Indicates inadequate performance on the competency

The use of a rating scale such as the one above can be improved by following these general rules:

- Do not allow a long time lapse between the observation of skill performance and its rating.
- A list of the observable traits which warrant particular ratings on the scale must be available to both the student and the evaluator.
- Remain impersonal and clinical during the observation and rating period.
- Use more than one observer if possible.

POWER TOOL INSTITUTE, INC.

Illustration 26. The proper care and storage of tools is one competency that is often evaluated using some type of rating scale.

Competency Recordkeeping

The effective management of a competency-based instruction system depends on an accurate record of student performance. The instructor must know precisely what point the student is at in the pursuit of occupational competency in order to make full use of available instructional resources. The instructor and the students must have instant access to the results of an assessment of the quality of their performance. Two basic types of competency records are recommended for use in a competency-based program:

Progress charts

Progress records

Progress Charts. This familiar device is primarily a management tool that can be used by the instructor to determine instantly how each student is progressing in the acquisition of the prestated competencies. This record commonly appears as a wall chart (see Illustration 6). The left-hand column of the progress chart, or Competency Record Wall Chart as shown in Illustration 27, contains space for the names of the students in the class. The top section of the progress chart should contain abbreviated statements, or unit titles, for various competencies that the student must acquire in order to be occupationally proficient. When the student has attained competence in a particular skill the box is completely shaded. Typically, a skill in which the student is developing proficiency, or a unit that has been introduced, is represented by a box that is half-shaded diagonally.

A sample version of a Competency Record Wall Chart is shown in Illustration 27.

The instructor can determine from this chart, for example, that one student, Donald Peterson, is doing rather well in the pursuit of competency. Two students, James Watson and Harold Denning, are having difficulty in achieving the required score on the safety examination and have not progressed any further. On the other hand, John Jones and Maria Sanchez are at least attempting to gain other proficiencies which can be introduced prior to their gaining total competency in safety. Progress charts are useful devices which help in the management of instruction. They, however, do not supply all the detailed information that the instructor may need.

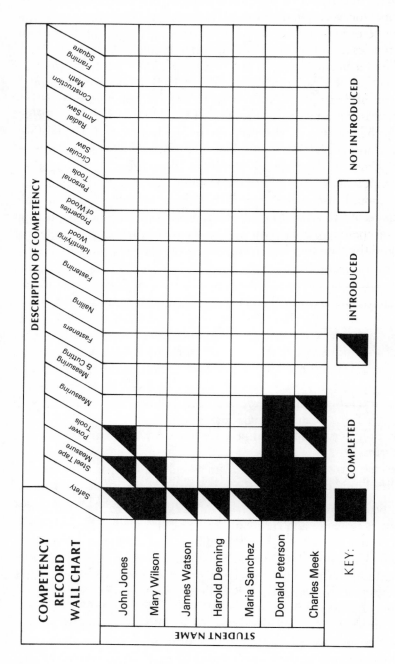

Illustration 27. The Competency Record Wall Chart in use.

Progress Records. This type of document can be thought of as a transcript for vocational-technical instruction. The format of the progress record should allow space for tracking the attainment of all competencies as well as for recording other details. Shown below is an example of a heading that might be used for the "student information" section of a progress record. (See Chapter One for additional comments and samples.) Notice that in this example locator-type information is contained so that it can be used at a later time for follow-up. Another section of the progress record has space for recording objective and subjective evaluation. The power tools section of the "Developmental Example" is shown in Illustration 29. Progress on each competency should be tracked or presented in a similar manner.

One should also make certain that there is ample space on the progress record to accommodate the following information: unit title of the competency, minimum acceptable performance, the student's score, and the date on which competency was attained.

STUDENT'S PERMANENT ADDRESS:	PLACE OF INITIAL EMPLOYMENT:
Name	Name of Business
Street or Post Office Box	Name of Employer or Supervisor
City, State, Zip Code	Street or Post Office Box
Area Code & Phone Number	City, State, Zip Code

Illustration 28. The student information section of a progress record.

Grading in a Competency-Based Instruction System

Competency-based instruction techniques challenge the traditional methods of teaching and certifying student performance. Research that has been done on learning mastery indicates that a majority of students will gain skills and knowledge at the highest level if given sufficient learning time and provided with appropriate learning experiences. This is the foundation of competency-based instruction, or what is sometimes referred to as a mastery learning.

An instructor who converts to a competency-based instruction system generally accepts the philosophy that a student should be allowed to pursue competency at their own individual pace. Many secondary and

COMPETENCY RECORD FOR

JOHN JONES

(Student Name)

Job Title _ROUGH CARPENTER_   Unit Title _POWER TOOLS_   Date _____

	COMPETENCY NUMBER OR DESCRIPTION	MINIMUM ACCEPTABLE PERFORMANCE	ACTUAL STUDENT PERFORMANCE	DATE OF ATTEMPT OR ATTAINMENT	INSTRUCTOR'S EVALUATIVE COMMENTS
SUBJECTIVE EVALUATION	Bevel Adjustments	1/16"			
	Rip Cuts	1/32"			
	Crosscuts	1/32"			
	Saber Bevel Cuts	1/16"			
	Saber Metal Cuts	1/32"			
	Planing Window Casings	1/16"			
	Planing Door Casings	1/16"			
OBJECTIVE EVALUATION	Circular Saw, Safe Use	5			
	Freehand Cuts	5			
	Circular Saw, Advanced	4			
	Drill, Safe Use	5			
	Changing Drill Bits	5			
	Boring	4			
	Drill Maintenance	4			
	Saber Saw, Safe Use	5			

Illustration 29. The Student Progress Record in use.

postsecondary vocational programs, however, are time based. That is, students must develop competencies in a specified period of time and often student performance must be assessed at specified intervals.

Time-based educational systems are varied. They include semesters, six-week time blocks, quarters, etc. An "end" of instruction is characteristic of a traditional time-based system of instruction as well as a "semester or six-week's grade." An instructor who converts to a competency-based instruction program but is working in a school which requires the use of a time-based system has few options with regard to required grading. Under the time-based system of instruction students of varying capabilities are forced to reach competency within a certain block of time and the instructor must assess student performance over these specified periods of time.

An instructor who is working in a postsecondary vocational school which operates on a nongraded, open-entry, open-exit concept, however, will have little difficulty in assessing student performance in an appropriate way. In this system, standards are clearly specified and the student may be considered competent at the desired level of performance without regard to the time required to achieve mastery or the assignment of a label, or grade. However, an instructor who is working in a comprehensive high school, or other setting, which is time based and requires grading often must assign labels to student performance at specified intervals.

We have already noted that grading is incompatible with an ideal competency-based instruction system. Unfortunately, there has been little curricular restructuring so that schools can accommodate competency-based instruction systems. A competency-based system can, however, be used in a school which uses time-based evaluation and marking periods. The positive, goal-oriented characteristics of a competency-based instruction system far outweigh the negative aspects of having to assign a grade to competency attainment. Since the chances that you will find yourself in a situation which requires grading are quite high, we will now examine some of the options you have in a time-based system which requires grading.

1. *Convert to a Satisfactory/Unsatisfactory Labeling System.* This method is one of the best to use if you must assign a grade to accumulated student performance over a period of time. It is better to assign an *S*, for satisfactory, to a student who has tried but not met a single competency in the first 6-week grading period than to give that student

an *F*. The S/U grading system gives the instructor great flexibility and the student is placed under the least amount of pressure to achieve grades. There are, however, disadvantages associated with this type of labeling scheme. Students, and parents when appropriate, should know what warrants an "unsatisfactory" rating for a particular grading period, but this is difficult to do without forcing the assessment of student performance into some type of time-based format and this is, of course, undesirable.

Consider the example of an automotive mechanics class which requires the completion of a total of 120 competency units. A responsible instructor should design the curriculum so that most students are able to meet these competency requirements within the given time frame. Assume that there are six, six-week grading periods for which the instructor must assign either an *S* or a *U* grade. The instructor in this case generally has two options to follow. At the beginning of each grading period the students (and their parents, if necessary) should be informed of what competencies must be obtained in order to earn an *S* rating. The instructor must decide at what rate a student must complete the units of instruction in order to receive an *S* rating. The rate can easily be determined by dividing the total number of competencies by the number of grading periods. In our example 120 units divided by 6 grading periods gives us an answer of 20. Twenty is the total number of units a student must complete per six-week period to perform at a rate which would, if continued, assure completion of the course.

There is also another method which can be used. The total number of units which must be completed every six weeks may be based upon their relative difficulty. For example, it might be determined that the automotive mechanics students should meet 25 competency requirements in each of the first two six-week grading periods to receive an *S* rating. The rationale for this could be that the first 50 competencies are less difficult than the remaining 70. The instructor should then determine the exact number of competency requirements that should be met in each of the grading periods that remain.

The reader should always bear in mind that grading on a time-based system is undesirable in a competency-based program. The strictest limit this imposes is that students are not free to learn at their own pace. If a different method than that described above is used by the instructor to determine a student's grade when using an S/U system those involved in the process must know how the grade is to be determined.

2. *Assign letter grades which equate the "minimum acceptable performance" rating with a C.* There are many limitations which arise from equating minimum acceptable performance with a C letter grade. One of the more obvious deficiencies can be revealed by asking the following questions: "Does a student who has completed two units of instruction at the A level in a six-week period receive an A? If so, what does the student who has completed 14 units at the B level and 5 at the A level receive? The second student is closer to achieving the goal of being occupationally proficient but would receive a B in most cases because traditional grading techniques dictate that the student's average performance (B+) is the grade which is awarded. Is this fair? Most of us would agree that this method of grading is inadequate and that the problems and limitations are indeed vexing.

One alternative is to assign two grades for each six-week period and average them together using some type of weighting scheme which takes both the time factor and overall performance into account. One grade could be assigned for the total number of competency requirements which have been met and the other grade could be assigned by equating C with the "minimum acceptable performance rating."

Consider the following example. Assume that a student records an average performance rating of B on 15 completed units and that you want the rate at which the student completes these units to equal a certain percentage (40%) of the student's final grade. A grade can be assigned to the *rate* of competency attainment. To determine this you can use a traditional percentage point system that is associated with assigning grades to determine the grade. A scale like the one shown below can be used:

90-100%	A
80-89%	B
70-79%	C
60-69%	D
59% and below	F

The percentages associated with each of the grades can be applied to the total number of competency requirements in a job title curriculum.

We will use the automotive mechanics class as our example in this discussion and will illustrate how percentage points can be used to assign grades to the rate of competency attainment. Convert the percentage at the low end of each of the grade spreads to a decimal and multiply the total number of competencies by this number. The product of this simple calculation is then divided by the number of grading periods.

Decimal Equivalents	120 × % expressed as a decimal	Minimum number of units to be completed in each grading period	Grade
.90 and above	108	18	A
.80-.89	96	16	B
.70-.79	84	14	C
.60-,69	72	12	D
.59 and below	71 and below	below 12	F

The student in our automotive mechanics example who has mastered 15 competency requirements during the grading period would receive a *C* grade on the rate of competency attainment based on the table above.

Now, we must calculate how the performance rating of *B* is weighted with the rating of *C* to obtain a single grade for a six-week grading period. One method that can be used is to assign the following numerical value to the five commonly used letter grades. For example:

4	A
3	B
2	C
1	D
0	F

The students grade could then be calculated as follows:

$$.60 \times 3 = 1.80$$
$$.40 \times 2 = \underline{\ \ .80}$$
$$2.60$$

The numerical total of 2.6 could be rounded off to a 3.0. This would then equate with a letter grade of *B*.

There are serious limitations when using this type of grading system in competency-based instruction. People simply do not learn at the same rate. A true competency-based instruction system is designed to accommodate diverse learning patterns, and the varying capabilities of learners. Assigning a letter grade in a performance-based instruction system diminishes the underlying tenets of mastery learning but is sometimes unavoidable.

REVIEW QUESTIONS

1. What is the difference between the meaning of the words *test* and *evaluation?*

2. List and define at least five characteristics of an effective evaluation system.

3. How can a subjective rating be assigned to observed student performance?

4. How can the rate of student performance on competencies be assigned a grade?

5. What are the two methods by which objective evaluations can be made?

6. Write an example of each of the following types of test questions, using the principles discussed in this chapter:
   a.) essay
   b.) short answer
   c.) multiple-choice
   d.) matching
   e.) true-false

7. What is the most common technique associated with the subjective evaluation of competencies?

8. Why is competency recordkeeping important?

9. What is a progress record?

10. What is a progress chart?

11. Why is grading incompatible with a competency-based instruction system?

CHAPTER

Psychological Foundations of Techno-Motor Skill Learning

SEVEN

S KILLS instruction for occupational proficiency is an important learning discipline which the instructor in a competency-based instruction system must consider. Specialized techniques and methods that will maximize learning outcomes can be used with a competency-based instruction system. At the end of the 19th century, social scientists and behavioral psychologists began to do controlled research on the processes governing the acquisitions of skills. This effort continues in a somewhat limited way, yet even today much of the research is based on indirect data collection. What has been learned is useful nonetheless.

The successful implementation of a competency-based instruction system depends on the careful consideration and use of principles of techno-motor skill learning. In Chapter 1 some possible rationales were presented in response to the question, "Why should I use a competency-based instruction system?" One of the responses was that this type of learning system is a psychologically sound method of conducting occupational instruction. Therefore, a description of the basic psychological principles of techno-motor skill learning should be included in any discussion of competency-based instruction. Accordingly, we shall examine the following questions in this chapter:

What is techno-motor skill instruction?

What are the principles of techno-motor skill instruction?

What are the methods used in techno-motor skill instruction?

What Is Techno-Motor Skill Instruction?

Learning has been traditionally classified into three categories: cognitive, affective, and psycho-motor.

Cognitive learning is traditionally thought of as intellectual comprehension or "brain work." Learning how to solve mathematical word problems consistently is an example of cognitive learning. Another example is the ability to convert measurements which are given in eighths to sixteenths.

Affective learning is thought of largely as being attitudinal in nature. The consistent use of safe work habits in the shop is an example of an educational objective that is in the affective domain, or domain of values.

An example of an affective learning deficiency could be an irresponsible attitude toward the care of tools. The instructor should talk with the student and encourage an improvement in attitude. Evidence that improvement in the affective domain of learning has taken place can be seen if a change in the student's behavior is manifested. In this case, the student might, for example, begin to clean tools properly and to replace them in their proper storage location. The affective domain is probably best reflected in technical instruction in the area of personal pride in workmanship. Students' attitudes are reflected by the degree of care and pride they take in their work.

Psycho-motor learning, the third classification, can best be described as learning that affects the development of physical aptitude. An individual who has gained proficiency in hitting a baseball, for example, has learned a psycho-motor skill. The same is true of a student who has learned to make a freehand cut with a circular saw.

It is easy to list other examples that fall into the three domains of learning outlined above. It is also possible to point out several examples which might fall in a "gray area." A large segment of learning is difficult to categorize as being exclusively in one of the three categories we have discussed. There is often some overlapping. This becomes evident when the following question is considered: "Is occupational instruction predominantly cognitive or predominantly psycho-motor?"

We know that occupational instruction requires the mastery of some knowledge that is in the cognitive domain, for example, the ability to absorb necessary technical knowledge from reading or a knowledge of mathematics. How else could a carpenter compute tolerable weight loads for a span of floor, or be able to determine a detailed materials list for a large construction job? No vocational instructor would state, however, that occupational instruction is primarily cognitive or requires only brain work. A student who is preparing to become a rough carpenter, for example, would have to understand several functions of basic geometry in order to lay out a plot for a building site. This is an example of an application of cognitive learning. However, to become occupationally proficient, this student would also have to learn how to nail for hours without becoming excessively fatigued or hitting a thumb. This is distinctly an application of psycho-motor learning.

The occupational tasks required under the job title of rough carpenter demand the development of both psycho-motor skill and cognitive knowledge. A similar blend of interdependent cognitive and psycho-motor skill is found in most occupations. This is a prevalent pattern in technical instruction. The instructor in a competency-based instruction system must get the best results possible from specialized skills instruction by using what is known about the processes and techniques of what we will term *techno-motor skill instruction*.

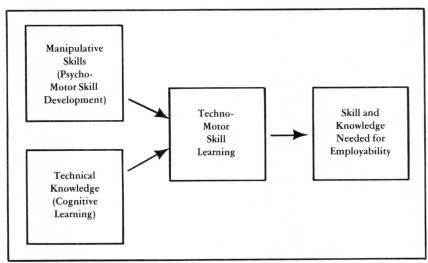

Illustration 30. The development of competency through techno-motor skill learning.

The types of learning necessary for occupational proficiency are predominantly cognitive and psycho-motor in nature. Most of the cognitive learning requires the acquisition of technical information; most of the psycho-motor learning requires the refinement of manipulative skills. The term that best describes the mixture and mutual dependence of these two types of learning is *techno-motor*. The following illustration graphically represents the relationship among cognitive sets of knowledge and manipulative skills that make up techno-motor skill learning.

The basic principles which promote techno-motor skill learning will now be examined. Instructional techniques for improving the learning results of a group of students attempting to learn an occupational skill will also be outlined.

What Are the Principles of Techno-Motor Skill Learning?

The following twelve basic principles of techno-motor skill learning summarize what is known about how to increase the effectiveness of techno-motor skill instruction. These principles represent a solid method of instruction for technical occupations, a method wholly compatible with the principles of a competency-based instruction system.

1. Learning is more effective if the student knows what must be accomplished before the learning process begins.
2. Demonstrations should be used when introducing a techno-motor skill.
3. The initial apprehension associated with learning a new skill should be reduced as much as possible.
4. Learning is more effective if it takes place in a setting closely resembling the actual situation in which it will be applied.
5. The learning of a techno-motor skill is promoted by providing immediate feedback to the student on the success of attempts to demonstrate skill proficiency.
6. The learning of a techno-motor skill is promoted if the practice sessions are interspersed rather than massed.
7. The learning of a techno-motor skill is maximized if practice sessions for the development of a particular

skill occur in different contexts.

8. Intrinsic motivation is more effective than extrinsic motivation in the learning of a techno-motor skill.
9. Proceed from the simple, prerequisite skills to the more complex.
10. Attention to errors in the early stages of skill learning can be detrimental to skill acquisition.
11. Provide a sufficient number of learning experiences to allow for the development of kinesthesis.
12. Multisensory learning experiences produce superior learning results.

1. *Learning is more effective if the student knows what must be accomplished before the learning process begins.* This statement fits almost perfectly with the basic concept of competency-based instruction. Few people would deny the basic logic and fairness of telling students what is expected of them. Students who are not certain about the point of a lesson spend most of their time trying to determine the purpose of the lesson or floundering in unpurposeful activity. The student's main activity in a learning environment should be directed toward attempting to master specific tasks.

Consider the following example of a competency statement for a small engine mechanics class:

> The student will achieve a minimum performance rating of ''4'' when demonstrating proficiency in adjusting the carburetor of a 2-cycle engine.

One of the activities that students might participate in to promote the acquisition of techno-motor skill is the reading of material related to 2-cycle engine theory. Learning is more effective if students know the reason why they are studying a given section of a book. In this example, the students know they will have to demonstrate skill in adjusting the carburetor. From their reading, they should learn that the skill which must eventually be acquired is to set the adjustment screw of the carburetor so that the engine operates smoothly. Learning would also be enhanced if they understood that they were reading a given section of a book to learn the theory associated with the mixture of fuel and air for combustion.

Occupational instructors must help students focus on the specific competency which is to be developed during every phase of the instructional process. Students must understand how the acquisition of certain sets of technical knowledge and skills relates to the overall process of becoming proficient under a specific job title. Since the time that is available to teach the skill is generally short, the instructor can improve learning efficiency by being precise in defining what it is that the student is expected to accomplish and why.

2. *Demonstrations should be used when introducing a technomotor skill.* For years a saying has been posted on the walls of many vocational classrooms. The author is unknown but the message it contains reads as though it came from a textbook on the principles of learning psychology:

> I hear and I forget;
> I see and I remember;
> I do and I understand.

The value of a demonstration of a skill to the students is stressed in the second line of the quote. Seeing a skilled craftsman or technician perform a task is extremely important to a novice. High-level, formative impressions take place in the early stages of learning a technomotor skill. This effect is enhanced by using well-organized demonstrations.

Special care should be taken so that the demonstration of the skill to be learned is appropriate and can be viewed by all of the students. The instructor who says, "Today we are going to learn how to mix mortar that has the proper consistency," should follow up that statement with a demonstration of how to mix mortar. The instructor should highlight the importance of using the correct proportions of sand and water by preparing one small batch that is too loose and another that is too thick before demonstrating how to correctly mix mortar of the proper consistency.

It is one thing to tell the aspiring chef that there are special techniques used in cutting food with a large kitchen knife. It is quite another thing to actually watch an experienced chef perform this task. The student who watches the chef speedily and gracefully chop onions forms a mental picture of the skill to be mastered.

Providing an excellent demonstration of the skill to be mastered is important. The student uses this mental image of the skill as a goal. The results of a student's own actions when learning a skill are mentally compared with the impression of the demonstration made by the teacher. The instructor's example is emulated and becomes a device for comparative feedback.

3. *The initial apprehension associated with learning a new skill should be reduced as much as possible.* Every step that the instructor takes in lessening the apprehension of students as they approach the learning of a skill is valuable. There are literally hundreds of different kinds of fears that an individual might experience when beginning a course of instruction. Identifying these fears is not a simple task. The effectiveness of the instructional efforts among a group of students will be seriously hampered if the instructor makes no attempt to reduce learner apprehension.

Probably the best way for instructors to identify students' fears about learning a skill is by recalling their own learning experiences. What were the fears or doubts that the instructor had when approaching the learning of a technical skill for the first time? This may help distinguish what fears the students might actually experience.

For example, prior to beginning a unit dealing with the basics of electricity and electrical circuits a student might be fearful of being electrocuted. One approach the instructor can take to lessen this apprehension is to teach the students about the safe use of electricity and the possible dangers associated with it. The instructor can then demonstrate how to safely use each of the devices and pieces of equipment used in the learning activities.

Every effort must be made to reduce the students' doubts about learning techno-motor skills. Otherwise, their attempts to gain skill proficiency might be hampered. When it is obvious that a student is having some difficulty learning a particular skill, the problem could very likely be caused by any one of a broad range of fears. Students may fear failure or may be apprehensive that their occupational selection was wrong. They could be experiencing pressure from parents or peers that relates to skill learning. Counseling or talking with the students can help an instructor discover these barriers to skill acquisition. The instructor should then work to reduce them.

4. *Learning is more effective if it takes place in a setting closely resembling the actual situation in which it will be applied.* This is a principle of learning that vocational instructors have used for a long time. When an instructor is helping to prepare an individual to work

in an office or machine shop, for example, the most productive learning experiences will take place in a simulated office or industrial-type machine shop. To use another example, quick, minor repairs on an outboard engine would be learned by students better if their attempts to perform this task were made while the motor was attached to a boat in the water, rather than on a test stand in a laboratory.

Expense, the resources available, and time often prohibit setting the stage for learning so that it exactly resembles what the student will encounter on the job. The instructor should attempt to inject as much realism as possible into the learning experiences of students. This can occur at various stages in the learning process, even at basic and elementary stages, but most instructors tend to wait until the later stages of skill acquisition.

5. *The learning of a techno-motor skill is promoted by providing immediate feedback to the student on the success of attempts to demonstrate skill proficiency.* This aspect of skills instruction is critical in a competency-based instruction system. Knowledge of the results of an attempt to gain competency directly relates to testing and evaluation. The student's attempt to perform the task specified in the competency statement can be thought of as testing. The student's and the instructor's assessment of the results of that attempt is the evaluation. The quicker the student obtains the results and the quicker the results are evaluated, the more effective the skill learning is.

Students must know how they have performed. They will make adjustments based on any shortcomings that might have prevented them from successfully attaining competency. This is particularly likely if the instructor provides careful guidance to the students on how they might improve. All learning activities in a competency-based instruction system should be organized in a special fashion to allow for quick feedback. An instructor, or a qualified observer, should monitor the performance of students who are attempting to meet skill proficiency. The memory of and feel for how to properly demonstrate a skill will be intensified if the positive results of this attempt are immediately made known.

6. *The learning of a techno-motor skill is promoted if the practice sessions are interspersed rather than massed.* The most effective method of teaching a skill is by not working on a single task for hours at a time. This can be achieved by carefully arranging numerous stra-

tegic practice sessions.

Teaching a carpentry student how to properly measure and cut plywood for constructing a residential subfloor can be used as an example. Ideally, the student would not work only on this task during the learning day. Sessions on computing the amounts of material needed, compiling materials lists, and cutting should be interspersed among other activities. Affixing the plywood to the floor joists should be a separate activity in which the student will participate after mastering simpler skills.

The process of building typing speed is also an excellent example of techno-motor skill acquisition. Typing speed can best be developed through skill-building exercises, however, other activities should also be included in the day-to-day effort to improve typing speed and accuracy. The use of several speed drills interspersed throughout one class session is more effective than making the lesson an hour-long marathon.

Concentrating on a single task or skill and practicing it intensively will often produce fatigue and disinterest. Students' minds will begin to drift if practice sessions are not spaced, and the efficiency of techno-motor skill learning will decline drastically. The instructor in a competency-based instruction system should manage instruction so that several appropriate occupational skills are being developed simultaneously. This is one technique that can be used to break up the instructional time periods into efficient units.

7. *The learning of a techno-motor skill is maximized if practice sessions for the development of a particular skill occur in different contexts.* The learning of a motor skill is promoted if the learner has an opportunity to practice the application of a skill in different types of situations.

Most hair-care techniques in cosmetology, for example, can be taught on mannequins which are commonly used in beauty-care programs. These mannequins resemble heads and are actually covered with human hair. Students master basic cosmetology skills by using these learning aids before moving on to the next stage of skill development. The next step, or different context, often involves performing the same basic tasks on fellow students. The new variable of a live person on whom to work definitely improves the quality of student performance. Next, the cosmetology students in our example might serve actual patrons in a cosmetology lab. This would provide the most advanced setting or context for skill development. This setting is close to what the students will experience when employed. This type of activity also fulfills another requirement of techno-motor skill instruction, the need for realism in an occupational instruction program.

8. *Intrinsic motivation is more effective than extrinsic motivation in the learning of a techno-motor skill.* Extrinsic motivation devices are grades, written evaluation reports, money, the threat of punishment, or the promise of a reward. The gold star that an elementary classroom teacher puts on the paper of a student who has spelled all of the words correctly on a spelling test is another example of extrinsic motivation. Intrinsic motivation is a desire or a wish to perform which comes from within an individual. A student who wants to master a skill at a specific performance level is intrinsically motivated. It can be thought of as self-motivation.

An instructor can better understand what motivates students by talking with them. The instructor may then be able to capitalize on the student's intrinsic motivations to aid in the skill learning process.

Intrinsic motivation is used when a nursing instructor explains to student nurses that the reason they must practice the conversion of decimals and fractions is that they must be precise in using units of measure to dispense medications. They probably would be told that a miscalculation in the administration of medicines could result in the death of a patient. More than likely, the student nurse would then make an effort to gain competency in the mathematics required. It is assumed that the student is intrinsically motivated to care about the lives of fellow human beings.

The instructor must determine what intrinsically motivates students and then use this knowledge to structure learning experiences. Capitalize on the students' inner desires. Explain the purpose of specific lessons, competencies, or tasks, so that the students can evaluate which aspects of the skills acquisition process are important to them in fulfilling their goals.

9. *Proceed from the simple, prerequisite skills to the more complex.* The instructor should begin the student's instructional program with the simple skills. Once these are mastered, the student can progress to more sophisticated levels of technical knowledge and manipulative skill. Learning would be hampered if mastery of the

more complex skills were required in the early stages of the learning process.

An example of not following the simple-to-complex principle of techno-motor skill instruction is to require a typing student to produce a mailable letter before the student has learned the keyboard. Proper stroking techniques, key location, the development of minimal typing speed, and knowledge of basic letter styles must all be mastered before the complex skill of producing a mailable letter should be attempted.

Although this example is somewhat extreme, the reader should realize that this principle applies directly to virtually all occupational instruction. The instructor must organize learning experiences effectively so that the student will be attempting to master sets of skills and knowledge which are simpler than those which will be attempted next.

10. *Attention to errors in the early stages of skill learning can be detrimental to skill acquisition.* This principle is probably one of the most difficult to adhere to. Most instructors instinctively correct students when errors are observed and explain to them the nature of their mistakes. The important thing to remember is that mistakes resulting from unrefined motion that do not jeopardize the safety of students should not be pointed out in the very early stages of techno-motor skill learning. They are natural occurrences. To highlight them in a critical manner may inhibit skill development.

The instructor should be guiding the work of the student in the initial stages of skill development rather than pointing out errors and saying, "This is what you did wrong." The more manipulative the skill to be learned, the more important it is that this principle be observed. Student apprehension about the entire process of techno-motor skill learning will be heightened if the instructor points out every error the student makes in the early stages.

Demonstrate the correct way to perform the task. Tell the students that they can improve their performance by doing a task in a particular manner, rather than pointing out that the students' early attempts were faulty. The students are already aware that they have not succeeded, particularly if the instructor has used effective demonstration techniques before the students begin the hands-on phase of skills instruction. Students need the instructor's guidance in the early stages of refining skilled motion, not criticism.

11. *Provide a sufficient number of learning experiences to allow for the development of kinesthesis.* Kinesthesis, or the automatization of responses, plays an important role in the learning of a techno-motor skill.

Learning to make a finger curl for a permanent wave properly, for example, depends on a high state of well-integrated kinesthetic cues. The example used in an earlier chapter of proficiency in making a freehand cut with a circular saw also depends on kinesthesis.

Educational psychologists explain kinesthesis as the process by which we become aware of distance and depth. Kinesthesis depends on the mutual cooperation and coordination of vision, touch, and locomotion. Kinesthesis has even been called "muscular memory."

A typist who has learned to type without looking at the keys has used kinesthetic feedback during the learning process to develop automatic responses. The same holds true for other manipulative skills which become automatized. Slicing meat, administering an injection, buttering a brick, cutting materials, using a router to shape letters, walking beams, etc., are all examples of occupational skills in which an individual can become kinesthetically proficient.

For each field of employment, the instructor ought to identify the skills that should become automatic. Then, an effort should be made to provide the students with as many learning activities as possible, so that kinesthesis can be brought into play in perfecting complex occupational skills.

12. *Multisensory learning experiences produce superior learning results.* The more often you employ devices or techniques that require the use of more than one of the human senses, the more you will help students learn techno-motor skills. Integrating sight, hearing, touch, and smell in the learning of a particular skill or task should produce superior results. However, creating learning experiences which enlist all of those senses is difficult.

Writing a computer program and submitting it to the computer center to be run provides only a limited amount of sensory stimuli; the student has used only one or two senses. The student who goes to a data processing center and types up a deck of punch cards, however, receives the added stimulation of interfacing with part of the data processing cycle and is therefore engaging in a superior learning activity. The learning which results from this activity will be committed deeper into the student's memory than if one of the employees of the computer center had prepared the deck and executed the program. This principle is what makes hands-on instruction desirable.

This principle holds true for the learning of any occupational skill. The more varied the stimuli that are introduced into the learning situation, the more efficient the resulting techno-motor skill learning will be. All or any combination of the 12 principles listed above can be applied to the teaching of techno-motor skills. We will now examine some specific methods and techniques that can help the instructor incorporate these principles when developing techno-motor skill instruction for specific occupational competencies.

Illustration 31. Monitors are often used to permit a large number of students to view a demonstration at the same time.

ELECTRONICS-INTERACTIVE
LECTURE GUIDE

Date_____   Student Name_____

Unit_____   Competency_____

Listen for the key points of the presentation. They will be presented in the same order as the questions on this Interactive Lecture Guide. Answer the questions in your own words.

1. What is force?

2. What is work?

3. What is the formula for computing work?

4. What is power?

5. What is the unit in which work is measured?   _____

6. What is the unit in which power is measured?   _____

7. List the methods of generating electricity.

8. What is the difference between alternating current and direct current?

9. What is the formula for computing amperage?

10. What is meant by the term "cycle" when speaking of electricity?

Illustration 32. An Interactive Lecture Guide.

What Are the Methods Used in Techno-Motor Skill Instruction?

The term *techno-motor skill* refers to a proficiency that requires an integrated combination of cognitive knowledge and manipulative expertise. Various methods and techniques can be used to promote the acquisition of techno-motor skills in a very effective manner. The following discussion is an outline of methods that capitalize on the principles of techno-motor skill learning. These methods include:

Interactive Lecture Guides
Lecture/Demonstration
Audiovisual methods
Multimedia lecture
Task simulation
Work station simulation
Projects
Student employment

Interactive Lecture Guides

A traditional lecture tends to impede the process of skills acquisition. Most instructors in occupational programs feel that the quicker students get into the hands-on phase of a project, the sooner "real learning" takes place. While it is true that most of the skills that must be developed by students before they are considered employable is done through hands-on manipulation, the nature of techno-motor skill learning requires that a certain amount of cognitive learning be mastered. The Interactive Lecture Guide is one device that can help students gain this cognitive knowledge without a great loss of interest.

The Interactive Lecture Guide is a handout sheet with questions written on it. The questions are written by the instructor and are keyed to the subject matter of the lecture. The student listens to the lecture or presentation and answers the questions, in writing, on the Interactive Lecture Guide. This device helps maintain the students' attention and focuses it on important points in the presentation. This instructional device also uses a multi-sensory approach to skills instruction.

Care must be taken so that the Interactive Lecture Guide is structured around key points of the lesson. Ideally, this information should include prerequisite knowledge that the student must have before moving on to more advanced skills and knowledge. An example of an Interactive Lecture Guide is shown in Illustration 32.

Notice how the Interactive Lecture Guide structures the presentation to involve the student in more than just sitting and listening (multisensory learning).

The Interactive Lecture Guide can also be used as the basis for a student notebook. The lecture guides may be kept by the students for future reference and study.

Lecture/Demonstration

The emphasis here should be on the word *demonstration*. This technique is very effective for teaching techno-motor skills, and often is a good means to use in the beginning stages of the development of occupational proficiency.

The instructor should list either on the blackboard or in a handout the key information the student should acquire from the lecture/demonstration. The student should be told how the demonstration relates to the overall goal of becoming employable and why it is important for the student to acquire the degree of skill that is to be demonstrated. In the lecture/demonstration the instructor should point out the highly refined manipulations that represent a standard of employability and should present the necessary cognitive knowledge. Doing this will help the student make relevant observations.

The demonstration should be clearly visible to all students. Nothing is more frustrating to a student than to have an instructor do a good job of stimulating interest in a demonstration before it begins and then to proceed while only a portion of the students have a clear view of the demonstration. A particularly good approach is to allow the students to participate and gain some hands-on experience with what was demonstrated. The lecture/demonstration is most effective just prior to the student's first attempt at lower order hands-on skill development.

Examples of appropriate lecture/demonstration topics for various types of occupations are:

How to roll hair
How to strike a welding torch safely
How to use the car lift properly

How to stir fry vegetables in a wok
How to use a computerized typesetting machine
How to wire a service entrance
How to strip a wire of its insulation

There are literally thousands of examples of lecture/demonstration topics for occupational fields. Some points to remember are:

- Tell the students, in detail, what is being demonstrated.
- Include a statement of why it is important that they learn a specific skill.
- Make sure that each student can view the demonstration.
- Highlight refined motions and knowledge that are critical in performing the task so that the student comprehends the standard of employability to be met.

Audiovisual Materials

The instructor will quickly learn the value of a multimedia approach in a competency-based instruction system because this system requires a highly individualized form of instruction. The very nature of how individuals learn dictates that most of the students will be at different levels of learning at any one point in time. This is both the blessing and the curse of a competency-based system. The instructor has two choices: either make all of the students fulfill each competency requirement during the same time period and wait for the stragglers, or allow the students to learn at their own rates. One way to effectively achieve the latter is to employ a variety of audiovisual materials.

Audiovisual materials such as tapes, slides, transparencies, slide/tapes, film loops, filmstrips, videotapes, and 16mm films may be used. Students can work on as many lessons as media and equipment for support allow. Each of the media resources used in a competency-based instruction system *must* be tied directly to the development of a specific competency and eventually to a testing instrument for evaluation.

Instructors should familiarize themselves with the multitude of audiovisual material that is available and choose that which is most appropriate for use in their program. Instructor-produced audiovisual materials are also very effective, but the instructor who is embarking on the development of a competency-based instruction system has to devote many hours to curriculum revision and the time and energy necessary to produce audiovisual materials might be used more valuably elsewhere.

One plentiful source of inexpensive audiovisual materials is manufacturers' training films and film loops. The instructor should make every effort to obtain these resources directly from manufacturers. School librarians also have access to numerous sources of free and inexpensive materials that are available to occupational instructors.

Multimedia Lecture

Lectures can be made far more interesting and effective by the use of auxiliary media. More sensory stimuli can be incorporated into the learning situation with a multimedia approach. Transparencies, slides, and 16mm films are best suited to complement lectures, since they provide visual reinforcement for what is being presented verbally.

Media aids should be used only for the purpose of promoting the development of a specific competency—they should facilitate the acquisition of a particular skill or set of skills and knowledge. Media aids should visually represent particular points that are being stressed in the lecture.

An excellent example of how a multimedia lecture can be used is in the identification of certain species of flowers. The instructor would lecture about the major classifications of flowers, ask the students questions about the reading that they have done, and show a slide presentation on the various classifications of flowers. The next step could then be to take the students to a greenhouse and show them the various classifications of live flowers. This combination approach can be highly effective.

Task Simulation

Unique tasks are associated with various occupations. The stage can be set for the development of proficiency in these tasks through simulation. Task simulation can be thought of as the student's opportunity to perfect a set of procedures that are required for employment. Examples of task simulations are:

The duplication and collating of a 50-page report for a printing program

Performing preventive maintenance on a piece of fire-fighting equipment

Maintaining a patient's medical chart

Mixing insecticides in their proper proportions

Making travel arrangements and an itinerary for an employer

Before task simulation begins, the student should be briefed on the nature of the task to be attempted, and the student's acquisition of prerequisite knowledge needed to perform the task should be verified. Once these preconditions are met, the hands-on process of the task simulation can begin.

In the following example of task simulation the competencies to be developed are the safe use of the power lift and air-powered impact wrench when changing a tire in an automotive mechanics class. This is a common skill that must be developed by students who are planning to be automotive mechanics. The instructor can prepare students for this task simulation by using a lecture/demonstration. The topic of the lecture and of the demonstration would be how to safely operate a power lift and an air-powered impact wrench. Students may be required to read a handout on the safe use of this equipment and to pass an objective test before being allowed to develop the hands-on skills used in this particular task simulation. The finer points of how tight the lug nuts should be on the wheel and how best to remove the hub cap should also be covered in the lecture/demonstration. After the lecture/demonstration, students could begin to develop their skill in removing and replacing tires.

Work Station Simulation

One of the most effective methods for developing skill proficiences in students is through work station simulations. One important principle of techno-motor skill instruction states that the closer the learning situation resembles what the student will encounter when becoming employed, the better the results will be. Simulation using work stations represents the natural application of this principle in the classroom or shop.

In vocational-technical instruction, the primary setting for an employee when performing particular tasks associated with a job should be simulated. A "work station," the most appropriate terminology for this kind of simulation, can be a functional piece of equipment, a structure, or a static testing device on which the application of basic skills as well as troubleshooting competencies can be developed and perfected. A key distinction between work station simulation and hands-on experience, or "live work," is that in a work station the instructor can program and control the learning situation. Simulation should be used in the intermediate phase of skill learning. Learning Activities Sheets can be used to guide the student through the basic processes.

Examples of work stations that could be used are:

A building site for a rough frame house

An 8-cylinder automobile engine mounted on a stand

A series of partitions set up to resemble modern kitchens

The cockpit of a flight simulator

A replica of a hospital ward clerk station

A series of booths fashioned to include most of the wiring situations that an electrician would encounter

Virtually every area of occupational instruction can benefit from using this approach.

Projects

This specialized instructional tool should be used for students who have mastered most of the required occupational competencies. Students have the opportunity to perfect skill proficiencies in an integrated fashion by working on a project that requires a sophisticated set of skills and knowledge. The project should be designed so that most, if not all, of the competencies associated with a specific task are required to successfully complete it. The student should be able to work independently at this stage of techno-motor skill learning.

Examples of projects that might be used follow:

Building a set of customized bookshelves

Typing a lengthly manuscript which includes tables

The complete overhaul of an engine

The preparation of a seven-course meal for a banquet

The complete investigation of a staged crime scene

The printing and binding of a booklet

Student Employment

The most advanced method of techno-motor skill instruction is probably student employment. The instructor should arrange a learning experience for the student which includes elements of actual employment in the occupational field for which the student is being prepared. The key features of student employment are that the student is required to consistently demonstrate, in real employment situations, job skills sufficient for employability. The student must make decisions and function as an entry-level employee. The instructor might still control the amount and type of work the student does and various circumstances with which the student is confronted. The student, however, is required to make employment-type decisions and should attempt to meet the standard of employability on all tasks which are performed.

Several student employment situations are listed below:

Assigning the student to work under a specific job title in a laboratory or shop

Arranging for part-time employment in the community and for related instruction on campus under the supervision of the in-instructor

Arranging for full-time employment in the community under the supervision of the instructor

Students should be fully prepared to meet the task requirements that they encounter on the job. Instructors must realize that this phase of training is only for advanced students who have met all of their competency requirements. The student will integrate all previously learned knowledge and skills by applying them to new situations and attempting to maintain the standard of employability.

The instructor is advised to draw up training agreements or contracts with the student and employer during this phase of training. This form of instruction is somewhat unconventional and all contingencies should be covered (i.e., unemployment compensation payments, fringe benefits, the grading system to be used, and attendance requirements).

REVIEW QUESTIONS

1. What is meant by the term *techno-motor skill instruction?*

2. Give an example of a techno-motor skill.

3. Why is it desirable to describe skill proficiencies to students before beginning the instructional process?

4. Why is it important to use sound demonstration techniques in the early stages of teaching a techno-motor skill?

5. Which principle of techno-motor skill instruction pertains to the concept of simulation?

6. Why is immediate feedback important to techno-motor skill instruction?

7. How does learner apprehension relate to the principles of techno-motor skill instruction?

8. What is the effect of spaced practice sessions versus massed practice sessions in techno-motor skill learning?

9. How does the use of different contexts affect the outcome of techno-motor skill learning?

10. What is the difference between intrinsic and extrinsic motivation?

11. Should the instructor point out manipulative errors made by the student in the early stages of the techno-motor learning process? Why or why not?

12. What is kinesthesis and how does it relate to techno-motor skill instruction?

13. What is meant by a multisensory learning experience?

14. Describe, in your own words, what an Interactive Lecture Guide is.

15. Why is the use of audiovisual materials important to techno-motor skill instruction?

16. What method of techno-motor skill instruction is considered the most advanced and why?

Annotated Bibliography

Alabama State Department of Education. *Developing Performance Objectives and Criterion-Referenced Measures for Performance-Based Instruction in Vocational Education*. Montgomery: Division of Vocational Education, 1978.

This report was designed to provide guidance for an instructor developing performance objectives and criterion-referenced measures. The relationship of criterion-referenced measures to the overall occupational instruction process is shown. A model for the development of competency curriculums is presented. Task analysis is introduced and explained, and guidelines for writing performance-based objectives are given. The nature of competencies and the evaluation of their attainment is also covered. The designer of a competency-based instruction system would profit from the suggestions made in the area of development, testing, and evalution of specific occupational competencies.

_____. *Performance-Based Instruction Curriculum Development in Vocational Education*. Montgomery: Division of Vocational Education and Community Colleges.

This report is based on information from many sources. The following major headings are included which could be useful to those planning to reshape an occupational curriculum into a competency-based one: Forces Contributing to Curriculum Change in Vocational Education, The Concept of Curriculum Response to Change, The Development of Performance-/Competency-Based Education, and Performance-Based Education in Alabama. Many sophisticated resources were used in compiling this report, which could serve as a useful appendix for further research in competency-based education.

Alabama Vocational and Technical Education Research Coordinating Unit. *Designing Education Learning from Task Analysis*. Montgomery: Alabama State Department of Education, Division of Vocational Education, July 1976.

This is a report on a project designed to develop realistic and valid performance-based curriculum materials for selected occupational programs. Various comprehensive competency curricula are reported. A model for an integrated approach to competency curriculum development is presented. The writer of a competency-based curriculum could use many of the ideas, methods, and techniques used by the project staff in the development of their materials.

Blank, William E. "Competency-Based Education: Is It Really Better?" *School Shop* 39, No. 8, April 1980, pp. 31-34.

This article discusses competency-based instruction and examines its four features. The author explores the competency movement as an outgrowth of "mastery learning." Numerous research notations related to the effects of competency-based instruction on learning are included. Three conclusions are drawn from the review of the research material. The article ends with a discussion of the advantages of a competency-based approach to occupational instruction and why more educators have not adopted it.

Bormuth, John R. "Feasibility of Criterion-Referenced Testing and Evaluation." A paper presented at the annual meeting of the American Educational Research Association, 1978.

The feasibility of criterion-referenced tests depends on two concepts: that bias can be controlled from test to test; and that one mental process measured by such tests may interact with another. Testing cannot be done reliably with criterion-referenced materials unless the first concept is active; and the usefulness of any competency-based measures is questionable unless the second principle is active. This paper is quite advanced and discusses the efficacy of using competency-based instruction materials. Sophisticated analysis techniques conclude that cutting scores may be rationally determined and that statistically generated criterion-referenced test scores may be developed to measure significant outcomes.

Braden, Paul V., and Paul, Krishan K. *Occupational Analysis of Education Planning*. Columbus, Ohio: Charles E. Merrill Publishing Company, 1975.

This comprehensive book deals with occupational analysis as a process of identifying and organizing that part of a vocational curriculum which is relevant to targeted performance situations. The planning process for the development of an occupational curriculum is discussed in detail. Techniques for conducting occupational analyses are presented. A comprehensive index and bibliographies are presented which may be of use to the writer of a competency-based curriculum.

Burger, Laura J., et al. *Competency-Based Route to Vertical Curriculum Articulation*. Minneapolis: Minnesota Research Coordinating Unit for Vocational Education, 1975.

This report was developed to aid in the implementation of competency-based curriculums in Minnesota and includes responses to numerous critical questions which may be of use to the developer of a competency-based instruction system. Among them are: What is competency-based education? How does a vocational program become competency-based? How can competency-based instruction help the student? What are the advantages of competency-based instruction? How can competency-based instruction be implemented?

Burger, Laura J., and Lambrecht, Judith J. *Handbook for Vocational Instructors Interested in Competency-Based Education.* Minneapolis: Minnesota Research Coordinating Unit for Vocational Education, 1974.

This excellent report is designed to help vocational instructors develop competency-based instructional materials. The organization of a local program, its contents, and the organization of instruction are presented. A six-step procedure for curriculum development is outlined. Useful guidelines for developing and implementing instructional modules are given. Methods of monitoring student progress are presented in a very useful form. The appendix is excellent as a further resource for the writer of a competency-based curriculum. A three-page bibliography is also included.

California Occupational Information Coordinating Committee. *Task Analysis: A Process Manual for the Development of New and/or Modification of Instructional Curricula.* Sacramento: California Occupational Information Coordinating Unit, 1978.

This manual is a guide for preparing new programs and courses for both secondary and postsecondary schools. The information contained is focused on maintaining or modifying existing programs to develop student skills which correspond to the skills necessary for entry-level employment. The manual provides the user with a uniform and systematic method for organizing current job task instruction. The manual is divided into four parts: Identification of the *Dictionary of Occupational Title* codes, The Development of Competencies Based on *DOT* Definitions, The Establishment of Course Content Framework, and The Development of Course Competency Outlines.

Chalupsky, Albert B. "Vo-Comp to Develop CBVE Measures." *School Shop* 39, No. 8, April 1980, pp. 66-67.

This article discusses a project called VoComp in which occupational competency measures are to be developed and field tested by the American Institutes for Research (AIR). The main objectives of VoComp are (1) to develop competency measures in 14 selected occupations, (2) to validate the competencies by field testing them, (3) to promote their use, and (4) to design and help implement a continuing program for competency test development. The general procedures to be used by the project are discussed. The article offers insight into the details of the development of valid competencies. The eventual use of the results of the project and a discussion of the status of the undertaking is included.

Clemson University. *Evaluating Students in Performance-Based Vocational Education Programs,* Module 6. Columbia: South Carolina Department of Education, 1978.

This is one of nine modules developed for use by instructors and administrators in vocational education. Selected narratives are provided on the role of evaluation, performance testing, evaluating cognitive learning through written tests, affective learning, grading, and recording. Three major types of performance testing and the six levels of learning are outlined. Objective tests and major records which can be used to chart student progress in a performance-based system are outlined. A glossary of terms is also provided. The module is written as a self-paced instructional manual.

Crow, Lester D., and Crow, Alice. *Human Development and Learning*. New York: American Book Company, 1965.

This book is an excellent reference book on the psychology of skill learning. Various sections are directly related to the psychology of motor skill learning. This book is highly recommended for the student or instructor who is interested in basing teaching strategies on the psychology of learning theory.

Day, Gerald F. "An Investigation Into the Use of Criterion-Referenced Measurement in Vocational and Technical Training." (ERIC: ED 115 933/CE 005827)

A review of the literature on this subject is presented and eight conclusions are drawn which have importance for the writer of a competency-based instruction system. The main area of emphasis is on the evaluation of student performance in relation to prestated criteria.

Deane, Arthur and Manuel, Donald. "CAP System: A Five-Phase System for the Development of Competency-Oriented Training Programs." *Adult Training 2*, Issue 4 (1977), pp. 30-37.

The article describes a five-phase plan for the development of competency-based training programs for adults. The five phases are: (1) the development of the profile, (2) validation of the profile, (3) specification of competencies, (4) preparation of learning resources, and (5) the establishment and management of delivery systems. Readers of this article would expand their knowledge of the sequential development of a competency-based instruction system.

Delaware Technical and Community College. *Academic Standards*. Dover (Terry Campus): Fall, 1978.

Academic standards for all occupational instruction courses on the DTCC campus have been designated in the form of competencies. Methods and techniques of grading and granting credit in relation to competency attainment are presented. Competencies for the following programs are included: architecture, civil engineering, business administration, accounting, banking, data processing, criminal justice technology, police science, electrical/electronics technology, and secretarial technology. Methods of monitoring student progress, specifications for how student performance will be evaluated, and the types of testing are discussed.

District of Columbia Public Schools. *The Competency-Based Curriculum: Developing a Mosaic*. Washington, D.C.: Educational Forum Proceedings, 1978.

This report is a compilation of opinions on the state of the art of competency-based instruction. Validation and monitoring of curricula and student counseling are discussed. This report expands the curriculum writer's perspective of the full scope of factors involved in implementing a competency-based curriculum. The section on counseling may be particularly useful.

Dobbert, Daniel J., "A General Model for Competency-Based Curriculum Development." Presented to the American Educational Research Association, 1976.

A comprehensive description of a model for the development of competency-based curriculums is given. The report is based on the presenter's definition of the word *competency*. The writer of a competency-based curriculum for occupational instruction could benefit from studying the flow chart used in the model.

Fraser, Larry, et al. *The Vocational Educator's Guide to Competency-Based Personalized Instruction.* St. Paul: Minnesota State Department of Education, Division of Vocational and Technical Education, 1976.

This report was designed to be used by vocational educators in planning, developing, and implementing a competency-based curriculum. Steps are outlined for the development of individualized instructional materials. The use of media and other resources is also included. Elements of the management of the competency-based instruction program are discussed. A bibliography of suggested resources is provided.

Gilli, Angelo C., and Wilcox, Lynne Moore. "A Critical View of Competency-Based Education." *School Shop* 39, No. 8, April 1980, pp. 44-45.

The authors of this article outline several of the dangers they see as being associated with a competency-based approach to instruction. They suggest that standardized curriculum based on minimum competencies might be the basis for providing unequal rather than individualized instruction. The authors also point out that the desirability of competency-based instruction is not likely to be established by sound research. The authors suggest focusing competency instruction on the needs of students. They present the view that competency-based education be used as a tool to improve instruction in conjunction with other effective techniques.

Giordano, Mario J. "The Non-Lock-Step Education System." *Project Summary.* Blackwood, New Jersey: Camden County Community College, 1975.

This project was an investigation of many individualized and self-paced instruction systems in this county. The report is a detailed document showing how to plan, implement, and operate such a system. Benefits are discussed. Systems as well as subsystems are discussed. The perspective of this summary document is focused, for the most part, on converting a whole school, rather than individual programs; to competency-based instruction. The overview, however, may provide the curriculum writer with information that has not been provided in other resources.

Herschbach, Dennis R. "Selection and Differentiation of Instructional Tasks." *Journal of Industrial Teacher Education* 14, No. 3, Spring 1977.

A systematic procedure for the development of job tasks through analysis is given. The author discusses how to determine what occupational skills should be taught as part of an occupational instruction program, rather than on the job. The article could be helpful in identifying broad clusters of skills and knowledge to be included under various job titles.

Hirst, Ben A., Jr. "The Components of Competency-Based Vocational Education." *American Vocational Journal* 52, No. 8, November 1977.

Competency-based vocational education is described as having numerous components: developing occupational inventories, instructional materials, and lesson plans; analyzing occupational survey data and existing materials; updating the task analysis; and making revisions. This is an excellent overview of the competency-based curriculum development process.

Hood, Florence F. "Coping with and Implementing CBE." *School Shop* 39, No. 8, April 1980, pp. 56-57.

The author of this article outlines the reasons why people resist change and thereby identifies some of the problems associated with converting to a competency-based instruction system. The instructor is shown as the key figure in implementing competency-based instruction. The general techniques to be used in competency-based vocational education are included. Several sources of CBVE materials are mentioned and an outline of a procedure for using this method is given.

Hughes, Ruth P., and Fanslow, Alyce. "Evaluation: A Neglected Area of Competency-Based Education." *Journal of Home Economics* 67, No. 5, September 1975.

This article addresses the concern that evaluation in competency-based instruction systems has been inadequate. The material is related to home economics but has value for all instructors developing competency-based instructional materials. The importance of using sound measurement techniques and of having a solid plan for the evaluation of competency instruction is emphasized.

Ingram, Maurice D. "Making CBVE Work at El Paso." *School Shop* 39, No. 8, April 1980, pp. 46-47.

This article reports on a competency-based drafting technology program at El Paso Community College. The article chronicles the development of a competency-based curriculum for drafting. The adjustments which were made for successful implementation of a system of instruction based on competencies are listed. Also included are excellent insights into the sequence of activities associated with designing a competency-based curriculum. The positive results as well as some cautions are included in the evaluation.

Jobe, Max, and Wright, Frank. *A Systems Model for Planning Vocational-Technical Education.* Austin: Texas Education Agency, 1973.

The development of a systems approach to occupational instruction material patterned after the Air Force system is the main concern of this report. The systems approach is based on four steps: (1) identifying the occupational inventory of tasks, (2) specification of course content from a variety of sources, (3) development of student activities, and (4) evaluation and follow-up. This excellent resource gives an overview of the entire process as well as useful ideas on structuring a curriculum.

Johnson, Charles E. "A Comparative Analysis of Three Basic Designs for Competency Validation." Presented to the Georgia Educational Research Association. Atlanta: 1977.

Three approaches to validation of occupational competencies are presented in this paper: (1) expert consensus, (2) product assessment, and (3) logical analysis. Each method is discussed in detail, using a model. The author concludes that each of the models is useful and that the choice of one another depends on the nature of the competency to be evaluated. The writer of the competency-based curriculum could use the information contained in this paper to help construct valid and reliable competency statements and to assess them after their initial use.

Knaak, William C. "The Anatomy of a Competency-Based School." *American Vocational Journal* 52, No. 8, November 1977.

The 916 Area Vocational Technical Institute in Minnesota uses a competency-based instruction system. The components of the program are described and discussed. They include curriculum development, grading, goals, advantages, and teacher involvement.

_____. "The Significance of Competency Testing." *School Shop* 39, No. 8, April 1980, pp. 48-53.

The author explores the problems which are associated with the concept of minimum competency testing. A clear distinction, however, is drawn between what is known as "minimum competency testing" and student competency testing or "Learning For Mastery." Parallels between LFM and competency-based vocational education are made. LFM is detailed as specifying required competencies, designing instructional units, and assessing progress. The author points out that LFM is a superior form of instruction. Research results on LFM are presented, and implications of the research findings are discussed. The author contends that according to research findings 85 percent of the students should reach a level of mastery in the same amount of time as *A* and *B* students under a traditional system of instruction. The purposes of competency testing in vocational education are examined. Methods of assessment are presented. Techniques which can be used to define mastery are also included. This is an excellent article on competency testing.

Lawson, Tome E., and Wentling, Tim. "Instructional Measurement Processes Considered Essential for Competency-Based Technical Programs." *Journal of Industrial Teacher Education* 12, No. 1, 1974, pp. 61-70.

This article outlines the various processes which should be associated with the competency-based instruction system. Information is contained which could benefit the writer of a competency-based instruction system in structuring, testing, and evaluating performance-based instructional materials.

Looney, Era G., and Finch, Curtis R. *Implementing Competency-Based Instruction in Vocational Education (Competency-Based Administrator Education Module).* Blacksburg: Virginia Polytechnic Institute and State University, Division of Vocational-Technical Education, 1977.

This module is designed to help the user develop the necessary skills for implementing a competency-based instruction system. Four sequential learning activities are included. Each learning activity in the module includes background information and is self-directed. The concluding learning activity is designed for use in an actual situation. This module would be of value for an individual wishing to do more advanced work on the implementation competency-based instruction in an entire school or department. Some useful information is included for the occupational instructor.

Mager, Robert F. *Preparing Instructional Objectives*. Palo Alto, California: Fearon Publishers, 1962.

This programmed text is an excellent resource for vocational instructors who are interested in writing clear and concise instructional objectives. Mager's style of presentation and writing makes for a superior instructional guide in the "how to" of writing what have come to be called "competency statements." This is an extremely useful resource for instructors wishing to convert to a competency-based instruction system.

McBrayer, John. *Resource Center for Competency-Based Education Handbook*. La Crosse: West Central Wisconsin Consortium, 1977.

An introductory orientation to competency-based education functions is provided in this report. A collection of essays is also included which explores the more speculative and complex aspects of competency instruction. Numerous citations of books, reports, and papers related to the philosophy, rationale, concepts, issues, and measures of competency-based education are presented.

Mechan, Merrill L., and Hoffman, Joseph L. *Organizing for Vocational Curriculum Development, Mini-Module Number 1.2*. Huntington, West Virginia: Marshall University, Department of Occupational Adult and Safety Education, 1977.

This is the second of three modules which are part of a larger set. This module is concerned with the identification of the various functions of curriculum development, and with the establishment of a sequential flow chart and time lines for developing a vocational curriculum. A set of suggested materials for the reader is provided. The primary value of this publication is to help the curriculum writer organize this task.

Merwin, Jack C. "Debate—Resolved: That Measurement Issues in Competency-Based Educational Programs Are No Different from Those in Other Kinds of Testing." Presented at the Annual Meeting of the American Educational Research Association. San Francisco: April 1976.

The paper underscores that evaluation and measurement issues in competency-based education programs are no different from those in other kinds of testing. The ever-present measurement concerns (validity of the criterion, adequacy of the sample, etc.) are the same for measures of competency. This paper is an excellent advanced resource on measurements and how technical measurement problems relate to competency-based instruction.

Michigan State Department of Education. *Performance Objectives Development Project*. Lansing: Vocational Education and Career Development Service, 1974.

This report examines a performance objective development project which was to generate objectives for all vocational-technical education programs in Michigan. An overview of how to write performance objectives is given. Recommended minimum vocational-technical performance objectives for the following areas are included: agriculture, distributive education, health, consumer homemaking, occupational home economics, office, technical, trade and industrial, and employability skills.

Miller-Beach, Audni. "DACUM: Identifying Competencies." *School Shop* 39, No. 8, April 1980, p. 63.

This article concerns DACUM, an acronym for *Developing A Curriculum*." DACUM is described as a method of creating a valid occupational curriculum. The article outlines the DACUM process, which includes the formation of a panel for the purpose of listing tasks associated with a field of employment. Further steps of DACUM are included in the article. The reader may also obtain additional details about DACUM from sources listed by the author.

Northwest Regional Educational Laboratory. *Alternative Methodologies for Competency-Based Education: The State of the Art*. Portland, Oregon: 1976.

This publication reviews the state of the art of competency-based education and covers various methods of structuring and developing competency-based instructional materials for use in the public schools. Various types of learning theories are tied in with competency-based systems. Methods of competency identification and instruction are presented. The strengths and weaknesses of the various approaches are discussed. This report is useful to an individual conducting research on how to proceed with the development of a true competency-based occupational instruction program.

Northwest Regional Laboratory Assessment Projects. *Annotated Bibliography on Applied Performance Testing*. Portland, Oregon: Clearinghouse for Applied Performance Testing, 1975.

This volume summarizes the contents of documents developed in the above-mentioned project. References are grouped by areas: concepts, development, application, applied performance testing, language arts, life skills, mathematics, physical education, sciences, and vocational education. Materials mentioned are available through the Clearinghouse for Applied Performance Testing. Ordering information is contained. The section on vocational education is useful as well as selected resources in some of the other sections.

Oen, Urban T. "Step by Step to a CBVE Program." *School Shop* 39, No. 8, April 1980, pp. 35-37.

The theme of this article is that occupational instruction should focus on job tasks and that competency-based vocational education is a way to accomplish this goal. Basic reasons why CBVE works are presented. The article describes how the Du-Page Area Vocational Education Authority in Addison, Illinois, has approached competency-based occupational instruction. This is an excellent article in which the author outlines a method by which the reader could develop a competency-based instruction system. The article concludes with a realistic view of the pitfalls of adopting a competency-based vocational education system.

The Ohio State University. *The E.P.D.A. Instructional System Design Training Project: Final Report*. Columbus: Trade and Industrial Education Instructional

Materials Laboratory, 1975.

This report examines an education project undertaken to develop a package of materials to prepare teachers to develop instructional systems based on task lists and performance, to construct a curriculum based on occupational analysis, and to apply the systems approach to the development of education programs. The value of this report is in the description of the modules, which focuses on systems and the systems approach to instruction, designing task surveys, occupational analyses, and the development of performance goals.

Oliver, J. Dale. "Measuring Student Competencies." *American Vocational Journal.* 53, No. 1, January 1978.

This article focuses on the three main functions of occupational instruction: (1) specifying job-related tasks in advance, (2) providing instruction in those tasks, and (3) measuring and certifying that students can perform prestated tasks. This excellent source presents the importance of competency measurement in a different light.

Peterson, Vance T. *Renewing Higher Education: The Competency-Based Approach.* Toledo, Ohio: Center for the Study of Higher Education, University of Toledo, 1976.

This publication contains 10 essays which present a number of ideas on what is termed as an emerging curriculum strategy, "competency-based education." The articles provide a philosophical base for the writer of a competency-based curriculum.

Popham, W. James. "Well-Crafted Criterion-Referenced Tests." *Educational Leadership* 36, November 1978.

This article gives the writer of a competency-based instruction system assistance in developing testing instruments. Emphasis is placed on how to develop competency-type tests which have an adequate number of items and possess reliability and validity.

Pottinger, Paul S. *Comments and Guidelines for Research in Competency Identification, Definition and Measurement.* Syracuse: New York Educational Policy Research Center, Syracuse University, 1975.

This paper is particularly useful in the area of competency assessment techniques and instruments for competency measurement. The identification of competencies which are relevant to life and work is dealt with. Even though the report does not directly relate to occupational instruction, the concept of how competencies are measured and validated is useful to the writer of a competency-based instruction system. There is also a brief discussion on the psychology of competencies.

Thompson, Sydney, "Competency-Based Education: Theory and Practice." *ACSA School Management Digest, Series 1,* No. 9. Burlingame: Association of California School Administrators, 1977.

This article presents evidence that indicates that competency-based education does produce significant educational benefits. Competency-based education theory is outlined. Data gathered from school administrators as well as from the literature on competency-based education are reviewed. This article would give the writer of a competency-based instruction system an excellent perspective on the implementation of a competency program.

Valentine, Ivan E., and Larson, Milton E. "Education by Objectives: Putting Teacher Accountability into Perspective." *Technical Education News* 35, No. 3.

This article discusses why teachers must insist on a validated curriculum that prepares individuals for securing employment. The article also emphasizes the importance of members of the community being involved in the process. The article is brief, but its contents are helpful from the standpoint of accountability.

Vincent, Roger D., and Cobb, Robert A. *CBVE (Competency-Based Vocational Education): A Study to Measure Its Effectiveness in Kentucky.* Bowling Green: Center for Career and Vocational Teacher Education, Western Kentucky University, 1977.

The effectiveness of competency-based vocational instruction is compared with that of traditional methods. Research on those involved in CBVE is analyzed based on self-stated goals for instructors in Kentucky. Instructional planning, impact on students, instructional management, professional development, and other program aspects are examined and commented on. Conclusions obtained from questionnaires on student performance, expenses of implementation, and the overall desirability of converting to a competency-based system are included.

Walker, K.G., et al. "Guidelines for Writing Job Profiles." *Balance Sheet* 57, March 1976.

This article focuses on the development of a job profile as a prerequisite for the design of a postsecondary vocational curriculum. The author outlines what are considered as the four essential points of the job profile: (1) environmental and organizational orientation to the job, (2) essential knowledge, (3) essential skills, and (4) desirable personal qualities. The article could be helpful to the writer of a competency-based curriculum in the early stages of conversion.

Washington State University. *Module 6: Preparing for Curriculum Evaluation.* Pullman: College of Education, 1976.

This module, originally prepared as part of a graduate curriculum for the preparation of curriculum specialists, focuses on the evaluation, development and implementation of a vocational curriculum. The module is divided into two parts. The first part concentrates on the evaluation process and the second part is devoted to implementing evaluation. Major activities such as assembling, analysis, interpretation, and evaluation of data in a school setting are covered.

West, Bill R. *Research for Performance-Based Vocational Education in Indiana.* Information Series Number Five. Bloomington: Vocational Education Information Services, Indiana University, 1978.

This position paper describes research goals of student-centered, industry-referenced, performance-based vocational education. Methods of strengthening the link between education and work according to manpower needs, articulation and accountability of the programs, the structuring of programs, and derivation of course content are discussed. This resource would help the writer of a competency-based instruction system organize the curriculum.

West Virginia State Department of Education. *Competency-Based Education: An Annotated Bibliography*. Charleston: Bureau of Vocational, Technical and Adult Education, 1974.

The materials included in this report were prepared from an EPDA project. Various occupational areas are referenced: agriculture, health, business and office, home economics, and trade, industrial, and technical education. This resource may be of some use in gathering specific materials for the development of occupational programs.

INDEX